THE BRIDGE TO HOME

*A SHORTENED VERSION OF
A COURSE IN MIRACLES
&
THE WAY OF MASTERY*

DENISA NELSON
MICHAEL CARLUCCIO
ANNE DIDOMENICO

Notes About the Authors:

Denise Nelson

Denise is a mother of three and a grandmother of two beautiful boys. She was married for many years, owned her own marketing research business and supported her children alone for years.

She started her journey to the Bridge to Home by studying "A Course in Miracles" in her twenties, then in her early 50's she began to hear and listen to the Voice for Love after studying "The Way of Mastery" ...

She now devotes most of her time to sharing her messages with others, extending love wherever asked...

She is honored to have had these lessons flow through her and she knows they will bring many wonderful revelations for our journey home...

She can be reached at deniseanew@aol.com and has a website at www.anewnow.org

Michael Carluccio

Michael is a 78 year old grandfather of twelve. He and his wife, Connie, have lived together happily for over 24 years. Both are retired from numerous jobs and professions. Michael's include elementary school teaching, college professor of psychology, contractor and writer. Presently they travel frequently, often visiting with children and grandchildren. At the present time, Connie teaches T'ai Chi and reads Tarot Cards among other things. Michael writes books of a spiritual nature and still manages some rental properties. He may be contacted at angelmichael69@yahoo.com

Anne DiDomenico

Anne loves life and expresses that in all she does. Her professional experience includes conflict resolution, mediation, teaching, writing, and project management consulting. She has worked in the educational, legal and corporate arenas both for-profit and non-profit organizations. Anne's passion is assessing and retraining the mind to bring about change in perspective, attitude and relationships. In her current consulting practice, Anne promotes self-leadership and resilience through spiritual intelligence. She is a wife, mother and grandmother who takes great joy in spending time with her extended family. She can be reached at anne@emergeconsultingllc.com

TABLE OF CONTENTS

Extended Writings:

PREFACE

Denise Nelson is the conduit for the 18 lessons given by Jeshua ben Joseph which form the central core of this book. Her claim is that Jeshua, in giving these messages, is the same energy that sourced "A Course in Miracles' and "The Way of Mastery." For those unfamiliar with these sources here is a very brief introduction taken from the official web sites of these courses;

A Course in Miracles

"The great classic work, A Course in Miracles, is devoted to teachings about who we are, our relationships to God and with each other, and the actually mental nature of our bodies and the world. There are three constituent parts to the Course: The Text, a Workbook for Students, and the Manual for Teachers. The Text lays out the theoretical foundation for the metaphysical system of the Course. The Workbook contains a series of 365 Lessons to be practiced daily for the purpose of retraining the mind and healing our perception. Finally, the Manual contains information for and about advanced teachers of God. The Course is also about miracles, which students understand to be, in part, a shift in perception to healed vision. But miracles are more than a shift in perception, because the shift has consequences in the world as we see it. The Course is a self study educational program for retraining the mind that is spiritual, rather than religious, in its perspective. Although the Course uses Christian terminology, it expresses a universal experience, and its underlying ontology is reminiscent of ancient refrains, echoing the world's most hallowed traditions."

The Way of Mastery

"This book contains the official extraordinary and transformational teachings of Jeshua ben Joseph who speaks not as a savior above us, but as our brother and our friend to gently and lovingly guide us to remember the Truth of our being. The 35 lessons in this book are a pathway to forgiveness, self-love and the acceptance of the perfection of each moment, and are designed to return the mind to holiness - wholeness. Jeshua speaks to every aspect of living in the world as Christ. With practicality, humor and loving direction, He points the way to the correction of every belief and perception that would keep us from knowing our perfect union with God. The only question left to be asked is: How much of God can you receive and then extend to the world?"

INTRODUCTION

The Bridge Home is an awareness of who you truly are as the holographic image of "All That Is." These lessons and the accompanying readings are this Bridge as it manifests in the 3D world. The "I Am Presence" you experience as you apply these learnings to your life becomes a knowingness that the Source of creation and all life is within you. It also recognizes that there is no separation, in truth, between you and me and all that appears in our world of duality. This is not a step to be taken lightly, for once the choice is made to come home to yourself all of creation will reflect that choice...you will be in the world, but not of it...

Denisa, michael and anne have joined with jesus in proclaiming to all the world that this is the truth and they are One. They share the fullness of the Jeshua energies as this One. Thus, they use the tools of duality to convey messages from eternity. These messages will be known as truth by many. Some may not be willing to accept them at this time. Eventually, all must choose the truth, since the truth is true and only the truth is true. If you are one who has made your choice to surrender to God's grace NOW, you will sense the truth these symbols convey.

Denisa, michael and anne with arms outstretched and open palms willingly receive God's unformed loving grace, and freely and joyfully commingle to form this love into the words you find here. Freely, they are offered to all. They openly receive these gifts of God in the knowing that all gifts received in grace and formed into a gift for others to receive will be returned increased a thousand fold to them. In sharing these words with all, they share the confidence that giving and receiving are the same. Their spiritual unity is manifesting this truth for all to see. All are invited to join into the warm embrace this truth extends.

The loving energies of Jeshua come now to you reading these words to awaken you to the truth of your "I AM Presence. When you choose to walk this road, you choose to come home to the truth of yourself: the holiest of unions that is beyond what could ever be "dreamed." This is your union of you uniting with your "Fullest Self."

The energies conveyed in these words are washing the windows of your soul. Any residue that would hold a seed thought that you are not pure and whole is being lovingly released and washed with the waters of home, our union as ONE.

Here, you will find 18 lessons of love which originally flowed through denisa. Michael and anne have accepted these channeled words of love as truth coming from the divinity inherent in us all. Modifications of form have been made, but the content remains untouched. Michael has added brief introductions to many of the lessons.

Following these 18 lessons, you will find the many conversations and comminglings of denisa, michael, anne and jesus. These represent our sacred heart singing its songs of love and dancing together with all. The messages these words convey are here for you to drink into your being. They represent the love flowing from our Source just as jesus symbolized this love in the wine of the last supper.... drink them in.... and be in communion with Yourself. These lessons are simple, yet, very powerful. For truth is simple, yet, you believe it not to be so.

Drinking in what these words symbolize, you now ready yourself for the shortened version of "A Course in Miracles" and "The Way of Mastery." These are the previously given words of guidance from Jeshua for our transformation out of the illusionary world of duality through the undoing of all the obstacles to Love; Love being the truth of what we are.

If you are familiar with these works, you will discover the same messages of love, acceptance and unity here in these messages from Jeshua/jesus. Each lesson is en-coded with love's vibrations. The vibration behind each word will be felt and realized. The seed of life carried within all will be opened leading you to the bridge home. This is the bridge home to self realization and is the only true journey you need ever take. All apparently diverse roads lead to only this one destination... this bridge. Whichever road you choose, whichever road rings true to your heart, will bring you to this bridge that leads to home... to me... the heart of love. With oh, so much love, Jeshua commingled through denisa/michael/anne/jesus

THE GIFT OF THE LESSONS

Three years ago, after having studied the Course in Miracles for many years, I went through some major life changes…It appeared as if much loss had occurred, all in a very short period of time.

I had a large market research company which literally collapsed. My home, cars, bank accounts and all that I owned on a material level left me.

On a personal level, a long marriage that had been full of turmoil finally came to an end, I had to walk away from the parents who had adopted me, and I also said good bye to many relatives and business associates…

There was a betrayal that took me to a very deep place one evening. I was crying on my living room floor and had wrapped myself up in a ball. I screamed out to God, "this place can't be real." At that very moment, I heard this beautiful voice for the first time, the seed within me that had lain dormant for many lifetimes cracked open, and I heard these words:

"IT ISN'T REAL."

I found myself without a car for about 6 months, and I remember one day looking in my driveway and hearing this voice say, "just bless it sweet one"… "simply bless it"…

A few days later, I was asked to sit at my computer and then the process of the lessons started to flow through me. I would listen, follow guidance and I was truly amazed and humbled by what I knew was coming into manifestation…

These lessons are very short, very strong and full of a vibration that comes through the words and the spaces in be-tween.

I have now seen many who just by having one of them in their hand have started the process of the bridge home to Self…

A lesson in allowance is the first experience that manifests and it begins the inner journey to trust. As trust blossoms, the soil of Knowingness grows and blooms…

It is an honor to share these with the world. All of your answers will come from the one within you, you will have need of no other… with love

`DENISA`

Message from the Heart of Love

As we move out of duality consciousness and move into a commingling with others, we experience what I am calling a "seamless sea of loving synchronicity." Swimming in this sea of loving synchronicity is what Jeshua asks when he urges us to see only love and be only love. Jeshua energies (the Heart of Christ) flow synchronistically through us all in this sea.

Here, there is no argument, criticism, correction, or disagreement... only allowing. Here, there is only seamless perfection shared by all. Here, sharing brings joy, laughter, peace, well-being and abundance for all who swim in love's purity of intent.

This is a place without rules... a place where only the loving randomness inherent in synchronicity rules... a place where meaning and pure intent to extend love join as one. This place, opened through random's door, now reveals a burning desire to know the unknowable... a desire that drives one to walk the bridge between duality and heaven. It is a place where you can do what you do and want what you want without planning and thought... being the light, being the love... only attracting love that is always about. Once this love is known, it cannot be undone. It is known forever.

Look for this synchronicity. Look for the sacred gene in us all. To find it, you must remember duality hides divinity. The

"Bridge to Home" requires your willing search, using only love, to see and experience. When found, fear it not. You have now become a catalyst who seems to lose himself while gaining all. You discover you are dearly loved beyond measure. Also, remember, love unraveling duality is learned for eternity. Love uncovered is eternally felt. This love uncovered spurs ascension. Yet, ascension comes from duality only with your permission to change out of duality into oneness. You must give permission for spirit to change your world. You must give permission for spirit to drive the bus of your human form with your former little self as passenger. This is but your human form (your mind-body) giving permission for spirit's sending your misbehaving ego child to the back of the bus.

You still know ego is always there, but it is no longer blocking your vision.

Through your willing allowing, you can now celebrate the challenge of duality. Allowing enables you now to celebrate all changes. With ego now acceptably tamed, sadness, fear, worry and drama are in the back seat. Loving synchronicity is now driving you with joy and with randomness.

Remember, also, the whole bus is connected. We are commingling, as wholeness, in our world of duality. So, any fear from the driver or passengers affects the whole bus. Calming love does too. So when seamless loving synchronicity is allowed to drive, the whole bus knows it. All celebrate with health, wealth and feelings of well being.

Your bus is not alone. When you allow unconditional love to blow the top off your bus, the whole universe celebrates your consciousness ascending. All on your bus experience a showering of loving synchronicity as they swim among the stars.

Know this as well: only ½ of 1% of humanity awakened to the power of loving synchronicity is the critical mass to heal our world and rocket our buses to heaven. We, here now, are invited to be part of that mass. We are all invited to the party. Let's celebrate in our commingling words and songs!

Written by michael as a celebration of our Oneness.

A Journey Home to Myself

Since early childhood, the desire deep inside me has been to 'go home.' When I called out to the heavens for help to make this happen as a child, the response I heard was always the same….. "not just yet, dear child, but in a little while. You have work to do, remember? Know that we are always with you..…..and one day soon you will be home again. We love you." And so.….finally 'getting the message'……I made up my mind to do my best at living on the planet and gaining some understanding of why people choose to live in so much pain. Even then, at some level, I knew life to be a choice and a wonderful opportunity to experience the new.

Growing up, I thought of Jesus as my beloved elder brother who was always there for me.……guiding me with great love. I knew I was here to do something but didn't know what it was. Yet, I knew it had to do with Jesus. For many years, I searched for a deeper understanding of spiritual principles and found within me a relentless desire to know these principles literally. The goal became clear: to manifest spiritual Truth through this physical form and through every aspect of life I encountered. I came here to live the Truth of I AM.

I've traveled a long way.....through many life experiences and profound personal relationships. Reading A Course In Miracles in the '80s and the Way of Mastery in 2007 ....with countless books, tapes, CDs, workshops, therapies and alternative encounters in the intervening years..... has brought me to this most amazing moment in time: encountering Denisa and the 18 lessons she channeled. These lessons have been so on-point for me allowing me easy access to the Now moment ongoingly. Life is unfolding into an ever deepening space of Oneness. These lessons express Truth in capsule form.......profound moments of thought in utter simplicity. For me, this material embodies the fast track on the bridge Home and am most grateful to have shared this project with Denisa and Michael.

Anne

LESSON ONE
Allowance

Allowance is the key to finding the Voice for Love within yourself.

When we allow we create a space for love to show itself... this is known as the gift of grace...

Allowance is a Key to the Kingdom.

It is the way; the means to undo the world of the insane (thought) that you have simply made in error.

But, before the insane world can be undone, practicing allowance, by making a choice to surrender for the allowing of what is, must be made first.

Let me say that by that choice you open the door to the truth of life – the Real world versus the unreal world.

It is not a choice to be made lightly, for in that choice you are saying (yes) to the Universe; you are saying yes to all of creation.

You will literally leave time, in a sense, and all of creation, a creation which, in truth, is neutral, all of creation takes on a new purpose.

Its purpose, once that choice has been made Is to AWAKEN YOU!

All of creation will reply... will reflect... Your choice!

Allowance in every moment is a choice to see all things as perfect, to accept and allow your every day moments to be as and what they are in truth, to pay attention in your now moments… to that which is in front of you. For once this choice is made, all that is in front of you NOW will be there to teach you, to nudge you, to retrain your mind!

In the practice of allowance, you begin to see with new eyes! You begin to see the beautiful Creation in all moments and all places, thus, comes the end of teaching. When the time for teaching is done, what is left to know…. what is left to do…. where are we left to go…. but to allowing all, accepting grace, ascending, being aware of the love of you for me, me for you, until we create with heavenly fun as one.

ALLOW ALL THINGS!

Do this practice for 30 days:

Just allow ALL THINGS.

Notice them. Pay attention rather then judge them to be good or bad.

Your judgment makes no difference, for all of creation is neutral and all of it has a purpose.

By making this choice of allowing, you have literally said to creation

TEACH ME ANEW!

So, enjoy every moment of allowance.

There are many treasures

There for US!

Peace be with you

You are loved soooooooooo!!!

Jeshua thru denisa

Each day you awaken from your slumber, consciously remind yourself to notice when you resist "what is." Then allowing the resistance to be what it is, ask for help in accepting what you reacted against and that you are resisting and judging as unwanted.

Do this faithfully for 30 days.

LESSON TWO

Jeshua asks us to get in touch with our desires so that we can experience the connection between what we want and what appears in our 3D existence. Eventually, we will discover that we are totally responsible for what shows up in this dream of separation we are experiencing. The truth of this revelation is liberating because we no longer experience ourselves as victims. This is the law of attraction.

Jeshua says that the reason we are to get in touch with our desires and notice how they manifest is so we eventually choose the one full and complete desire. All will eventually, at a time of their choosing, openly ask for this one desire that will contain all desires. This is the desire for the peace of God. This peace and contentment beyond understanding is without fear, without concern, without any chance of having it taken from us. This peace will be found even when all about seems unlike the peace you desire. The peace is within you.

DESIRE

Why desire, you may ask?
Desire is what fuels creation.
If you follow your desire, you are seeing how you are creating
your reality.
You are a GRAND CREATOR!
YOU ARE ONE WITH LOVE
LIGHT
ABBA

ALL THAT IS.
Therefore, I say unto you DESIRE is your engine!
It is your starting point for that which you will see in
front of you!

Begin to follow your desire.
Listen to that voice of your own desire.
Start with small things like,
"I desire to take a hot shower."
Notice as you take your shower how it feels.

Following your desire brings you to these feelings.
Those feelings are your true heritage!
So, begin to follow and notice what you are desiring!

Then, you may want to say out loud "I desire peace."
If you do desire peace now, then every morning for the next 30
days say out loud to this beautiful universe
" I want the peace of God!"
The universe is truly waiting on you to
decree this desire.

I desire peace!

Now, in the beginning once you have decreed that you desire
peace, You WILL go through a period, moments in your time,
where you will come to see all that you alone have created that
does not bring you peace. Notice these events; they are your
key to peace!
Honor and ALLOW all these moments that come to you to
show you how you alone have chosen unlike peace!
These moments will come
THEY WILL COME!!!

*They must, for in truth, you need to undo all that YOU have
created unlike peace in your life.
To do this, you have to see and feel all that you desire that
is unlike peace.
It is as if, when you choose for peace, you are bringing the
LIGHT to all that you have created unlike it.*

*For brief moments you will experience those things that need
the light to*

*bring them up. This is only so you can choose differently. For a
moment you may feel like this does not feel like peace,
GOOD
Here is your edge.
Here is where you get to pay attention!*

*Ask that which is unlike peace, "I seem to have created
something here that is unlike that which I truly desire,*

*How can I change this creation? How can I transform
this creation?"
That voice, your voice within, will begin to guide your way.
You will begin to undo that which no longer serves your
glorious self,
so that your desire, PEACE, can descend upon you.*

*That desire will help you to release everything that is
unlike peace.
It is the process of undoing the ego mind.
In its place comes your glorious self, light divine.*

*Peace will live in your HEART making it a sacred heart
A heart that lies next to mine, One with my heart*

ALWAYS!
It is our Sacred Holy Heart in ALL-WAYS!

So, LESSON TWO
D E S I R E!

For 30 days follow your desire for peace and all that is
not peace.
Carry on with lesson ONE,
ALLOWANCE.....

I love you so,
I am waiting patiently always, for your return to yourself
which is
Oneness with ME!

Blessings,

THE VOICE FOR LOVE,

Jeshua thru denisa

For the next 30 days, each day upon awakening from sleep, consciously ask for help to notice your desires and notice how they seem to manifest in your life. Also, keep allowing all to be as it is without criticism or rejection.

LESSON THREE

After 30 days of recognizing that your desires create your reality now is the time to accept what you have created fully. Surrendering to these creations is re-discovering your fullness of being. Let all of yourself in form be what you have desired it to be in form. Do not resist it even if it is no longer wanted. Resisting what is unwanted only has it persist in the form that is unwanted. Let it go by surrendering all resistance to "what is." Remember, "what you resist persists."

"Let it be!

Let it be!

These are words of wisdom

Let it be!"

Jeshua, the Voice for Love, speaks to us about healing our mind through surrendering to love in all things.

Also, we are reminded to remember always that allowing is the beginning and desiring is the engine.

Now we experience surrender as the comforter.

SURRENDER

Here, in surrender, your joy lays hiding.

Within surrender, there are many gifts waiting to be bestowed upon you.

Surrender is the gift package you give unto yourself that brings you home.

It is the giving of yourself, your true self, over to the ONE that birthed you.

It is the process of undoing all that you have created in error and in innocence.

For you must remember Creation is innocent.

So, for the next 30 days, surrender is your sojourn.

Bring all things to the ONE that Loves you eternally and only wants you to experience love, joy and peace in your life.

Bring unto me all of your feelings.

When you are feeling S A D N E S S, bring it to ME,

When you are feeling A L O N E, bring it to me.

Bring all things to me that YOU believe need to be healed.

BY HEALING, I am truly bringing you RIGHT MINDEDNESS!

All power, ALL TRUE POWER, comes from within the heart.

OH, not the heart that lives within your body but, THE TRUE HEART, the Heart that ALL SHARE AS ONE!

THIS IS WHERE I ABIDE WITH YOU ALWAYS AND IN ALL WAYS!

So, now, a little suggestion:

Close your eyes.

Leave the world of illusion behind you for a moment.

As you close your eyes, relax. Let go.

See your beautiful self, your light body.

Step forward from your earth body.

Then, gently allow ME to guide your light body down, down, down into the heart.

Relax. Come down deeper and deeper. You will know when you are there.

You simply will not descend any further.

Then, sit there with ME.

I WILL MEET YOU THERE.

Take my hand, sweet ones, and with the other hand give me your problem, whatever you deem that to be.

Imagine you are holding your problem on a golden tray.

Hand that whole tray over to ME, the love within.

You will feel a gentle spaciousness.

You may even feel a release, as if the problem has left your energy field.

Know that it has.

You have now given this over to LOVE.

Now, let it go.

Know that it is in the hands of LOVE and that it will be returned to you while you still remain in time.

All will be healed, corrected, made right for YOU!

Practice this always, however, for the next 30 days simply practice surrender every moment you feel anything unlike love.

That which stirs your feathers, so to say, bring it to the Voice for Love within.

I will correct your mind.

You will begin to see things through the eyes of love, your

true perception.

For, in truth, your perceptions of all things, coming from the thought of separation, have never been the truth of any thing.

So, allow ME, your Voice for LOVE, to correct them for you.

Thirty days

SURRENDER....

Peace be with you,

THE VOICE FOR LOVE,

Jeshua thru denisa

So, for the next 30 days do the meditation process suggested by Jeshua. Be conscious of letting go and letting God each time a problem seems to arise.

LESSON FOUR

Patience is only needed in the illusion we call time. In reality, all experience exists in the NOW. Patience is what brings us to the remembrance of this reality. Time is a device for breaking up NOW into past, present and future. Time collapses when we give our willingness to allowing all to be what it is, recognizing our power to have things manifest in our 3D world and surrendering to all that seems to occur in time as God's will for our good. It is this experience of NOW without past and without future that patience builds.

Patiently waiting for our desires to blossom builds trust. We learn with patience to recognize and affirm the unity of time in the NOW. With patience, we discover that desires are granted immediately, but because of a belief in linear time, these desires seem to take time.

PATIENCE

All of humanity wants things NOW…

When we first "open the door" to our Inner Kingdom…When we turn our attention to the God within and ask of that ONE to show us the way…we start the journey of re-membrance.

The journey is of itself an illusion… for in truth you have always been pure spirit. However, once you open this door to who you truly are, you begin a New Life.

Your ways of living life in your 3D world will become heavier, cumbersome and will not get you where you would like to be.

You must first be willing to listen! Then you must allow for that ONE who lives within YOU, who is guiding you every mo-ment, asking to take over the show. You must surrender to this VOICE for Love. Your way or the highway will not be your new now! Your life will be-come a journey into the world of pure, unconditional love...

Yet the road to it will be that road of undoing what you thought was life, in order to bring in TRUE LIFE.

Patience, patience will build your inner power for this journey.

The more you "wait on the Voice for Love"... the more you ask that Voice for all of your answers, for all of its power, the easier your life will flow. You will see that the "voice for love" is never in error, that you can truly trust that voice ALWAYS!

Patience will become the "Law of the Land"... the fruit of the tree that will bring you to your world of re-membrance.

That voice will always, always guide you to your right choice that IS the highest and best road for YOU at this time!

This is an inner journey. No One can be on this journey but you and your inner voice, the Love that lives within, GOD, ABBA, ALL THAT IS.

It lives within you now like a seed waiting to be watered and have some sun shine upon this seed, that "seed" which literally lives within your DNA.

It has always been so.

*And when you make the choice for LOVE… when you give up
on the ways of the small ego and let LOVE guide your life in all
ways PATIENTLY… then LOVE WILL BE YOUR NEW NOW in
everything and everywhere.*

So, patience and diligence for love, my sweet souls.

Allow all things…

Trust all things…

Desire only Peace…

Surrender to ME…

Patience…

Patience…

Patience…

*And love yourself for being willing to come home by taking the
journey back to yourself. Peace be with you always,*

THE VOICE FOR LOVE,

Jeshua thru denisa

Now, for the next 30 days, wait in trust for your desire
for peace to show up in your life. Allow your love to flow
to all. Surrender any separate desires to the one who will
transform them into creations to benefit all.

LESSON FIVE

Through surrendering to the will of God, you have willingly given up the need to have your little self (ego) try to control the life that is being manifested by you. This surrendering of control allows your fuller self to emerge. The artificial barriers between yourself and all else will dissolve and you will experience the "seamless sea of loving synchronicity" spoken of in the introduction.

CONTROL

As you practice allowing all to be as it is without correction, rejection or opposition, as you desire only for the peace of God, as you surrender to the grace of God in trust and patiently await whatever form this grace may take, you will no longer abide as a human being who even would "desire" to be in control.

You WILL COME TO KNOW THAT YOUR 'EGO' VOICE WILL NO LONGER SERVE YOU.

Through your process of allowing you will start to see that all things have a purpose. What that purpose is will many times not be apparent.

Your need to control your life, your family, your "world" will leave you like the leaves leave their branches in the fall.

It is a graceful process, as slowly you will come to see that, in truth, you have NEVER BEEN IN CONTROL.

It will be revealed through grace that life, has been living you all along!

As all things, this too is a process and you will come to love the process, for when you give up control, when you surrender to what is, when you let go of the "need" to be in charge of your ride on the track of life

YOU WILL BE FREE

AND YOU WILL FREE UP

ALL OF LIFE, as all minds are ONE. Every moment on your road back to yourself, every time you extend your love into this world you change your world as you open up a little space for those you love to be free also.

THIS IS SO!

You are all appearing to be separate yet your minds are joined as the ONE MIND in the Real World, the World of the unseen.

So, my sweet ones, every choice for Love opens up a choice for all souls, it has to be so!

So, instead of you driving the car, allow me, the Voice for Love, to direct the way! Put on your seat belt. Remember you are not the driver.

I AM THE DRIVER AND THE PASSENGER INSTRUCTOR AND YOU ARE ON THE RIDE OF A LIFETIME.

This ride you will be taking will be like no other ride you have ever known. It will be that ride that takes you to "heaven." And trust me, It is a ride.

*Once you embark on this ride the destination is certain.
However, there is no getting out of the car. Many times you may
want to get out, but the door is locked and it will not open until
you arrive at your destination.*

*What is that destination one may ask? It is the destination of
your dreams. It is the knowingness that only
Love exists.*

It is magical!

It is brilliant!

And it is the ONLY REASON you truly arrived here at this time.

*Let "control" be a word, a thought that flies out the window and
allow that which will come in to be the truth of yourself:*

PURITY of DESIRE,

SINGLENESS of PURPOSE,

COMPASSION,

FORGIVENESS, EMBRACEMENT of all,

FOR IN TRUTH THAT IS WHO YOU ARE

You are the sun that lights up the sky.

You are the stars that twinkle in the heavens.

*You are the ocean that allows all of its waves to cover the
shores with its waters of Love and ABUNDANCE.*

You are all of it. You have simply forgotten the simple truth of your being.

Peace be with you, for you are sooooo loved, my sweet souls,

The Voice for Love

Jeshua thru denisa

So, for thirty days consciously allow yourself to relinquish control over all that is in your life. Let your motto be, "Let go and let God."

LESSON SIX

Our emotional reactions are the keys to the undoing of the false belief that we are apart from love. Allowing them to surface, surrendering all feelings that are not coming from love to the Voice for Love within our mind, will allow healing of our souls to manifest in our world.

E-MOTION

Emotion is what holds you "in time"....

It is what keeps the "veil" between your world and the real world in place.

Your feelings are very important....

They are the life of your energy system.

Yes sweet souls, you are an energy system, you are pure energy.

Your emotions, if not allowed to flow, get "stuck".....

They literally get hung up in your energy system.

They cause dis-ease and depression and all the like when they are not allowed to be "felt."

Your emotions are your soul's way of talking to you.

They are saying about themselves and about you, "Pay attention to me."

They are saying, "Let me be expressed."

They are saying, "Embrace me."

They are saying, "Don't judge me."

They are saying, "Let me be what I am."

These feelings are consciousness too! Yes, all is consciousness,

consciousness being the movement of Love.

The air you breathe is filled with Love, consciousness, All That Is.

Your feelings are LIFE, yes, Life Itself.

They are your barometer. They are your guide to your Self.

They are to be HONORED, never judged, never stuffed, never
pushed away.

Allowance of your feelings will clear your energy field.

Allowance of your feelings will truly EN-LIGHTEN YOU.

Your feelings are "there" to be felt. They do not just appear
by chance.

You are a beautiful being of Divine Light. You are the Creator of
your world.

Allowance of your feelings is honoring your Soul, so my sweet
souls, as you "feel" you become alive.

Bring those feelings, all of them, yes, ALL OF THEM TO ME.

Bring them with-in. Ask of ME, the Voice for Love,

"What should these feelings be showing me?"

"What would YOU have me do with these feelings?"

The answer will come.

Go within, my sweet ones, bring all of your feelings to ME. I will, if you allow me, heal them. In truth, we as the "One" will heal them together.

Your emotions keep you bound in time. They keep you attached to THAT WHICH YOU PERCEIVE. AND YOU, MY SWEET ONES, DO NOT, IN TRUTH, KNOW THE TRUE PERCEPTION OF ANYTHING.

But there is ONE that does.

Come to me in your "unknowingness," even if you think you KNOW what a feeling is for, come to me within and practice NOT KNOWING. Admit you do not know what a single thing is or what it is for. It is in your not knowing that you allow ME to come and make right all that YOU have perceived wrongly.

I will bless you with KNOWING. You will come to know that you are perfect. You will come to know that all things have just been a misperception. You will come to know that what you think you see is not what is "real." Time and time again we have said,

ONLY LOVE IS REAL. ALL ELSE IS ILLUSION.

Your perceptions of life, your projection of what you think anything is or what it is for, is what must come to be undone. For in truth, there is only ONE thing going on in your earth world, it is the process of undoing that which has created your world. It is the undoing of that which your small egos show you to be true and, thereby, through this undoing bringing back to life that which is true, "Love."

ONLY LOVE EXISTS.

45

And YOU, my sweet souls, will come to know this in time by letting go of that which you think you see (surrendering all to the Voice for Love within) and allowing ME (LOVE, ALLNESS) to correct your perceptions for YOU.

Come to me NOW, for I love you soooooooooo.

30 days, pay attention to your e-motions and bring all unlike love to ME.

The Voice for Love

Jeshua thru denisa

LESSON SEVEN

The willing release of judgment in the world of illusion
brings Christ, the Heart of Love, back into this world
of illusion as each and every one of "you" offers this
willingness. This is the NOW of the second coming of
Christ, promised by Jesus.

JUDGMENT

My sweet souls, if you could only see the way I do from the
world beyond, you would know what judgment does to your very
beingness! It literally clogs up your energy system. It depletes
your flow. It takes you away from heaven, from peace, from love.

Judgment is the exact opposite of that, which you desire,

THE KINGDOM of HEAVEN.

It is a mis-perception.

It is YOUR belief that the one you see outside of you, the event
or the reality that you think you see with your earth eyes,
is true!

In truth there is only ONE.

All whom you see are you: an aspect of yourself. Would you
judge yourself, my sweet souls? If the answer is yes, this is
another mis-perception for you are never guilty, you are never
without truth. You have believed yourself to be that which you
think you see, a body, in form, on a loveless planet.

Nothing could be further from the truth.

The veil that keeps you from knowing who you are is that veil which shows you that the one over there is not you!

Yes, my sweet soul, your perceived separation from ME, the Heart of Love, has convinced you that you are not the ONE. Yet, I tell you now, that which you see is THE KINGDOM of HEAVEN. That which you see is ME.

That which you see is Love.

That which you see is You.

Your life, your very life, in truth, is perfect. You are perfect and so is the one in front of you. What you see in another that "pushes" your buttons is something left unhealed within yourself.

Nothing can appear in front of you in time that YOU, your very self, your fullest self, has not called to you. You can never be a victim! You are the creator. Therefore, what would you wish to see in front of you?

If you carry feelings of lack of worth within you, you will see those thoughts of lack reflected outside of yourself by those who seem to have no respect for you! If you carry within guilty judgment of self, you will bring to yourself those that would judge you as guilty.

You are the very thought process of your own life. If this is so, and it is, that means there is only GOD. There is only LOVE, a Love that is bringing to you that which you reflect from within. That is why I say unto you this is an inside job.

We are together removing all the cob webs that would keep YOU from knowing who you are.

YOU ARE DIVINE.

YOU ARE LOVE.

YOU ARE ALWAYS ONE WITH ME.

In truth, you are so enveloped in love, every moment in time because I, the Heart of Love, love YOU!

So, judgment my dear ones, is NOT of the KINGDOM.

Look again.

What is this one, this event, This appearance showing you?

If you cannot see what it is, bring it to ME, the Voice for Love Within.
Come within. Ask ME to show you the truth.

I will show you that which you have believed about yourself that would "cause" you to judge this one as guilty. Once you have found your treasure, that which has been brought to you as a gift with a beautiful bow, although it does not all appear as a gift at first, then, and only then give that treasure, that knowingness to ME, the Heart of Love. I will translate it for you. It will leave your energy system and be turned back into that which it truly is, Love, as all is Love.

I am the way.

I am the all.

YOU are one with ME.

It has always been so.

49

Love the one in front of you whether that one appears to be friend or foe. Love them soooooooooo much, for they are in truth a gift from yourself to yourself. They come to awaken you!

Judgment, my sweet souls, is out of alignment with Love. It keeps you from your peace. Judgment keeps you in "time." Time is not the real world, and our journey together is one of undoing time so that time, unreality, will no longer seem to be!

HEAVEN, LOVE, will be all that is left.

That is the Golden Era. This is the age talked about for eons.

You are here "Now" for a purpose. YOU are a part of that descension of Love back into this world of symbols, of illusion, of fear, of all unlike what YOU truly are. You are the second coming of Christ into the illusion of duality.

30 days, my sweet ones, notice your judgment!

The Voice for Love,

Jeshua thru denisa

For these 30 days each time you notice yourself making a judgment of anything or anyone ask the Voice for Love to help you see things differently. Then know that it is accomplished and wait patiently for time to collapse and for your judgment to be undone. It must be so!

LESSON EIGHT

Do you wish to change the world? Do you wish to experience peace under all circumstances? Do you wish to have joy without end? Here, Jeshua gives the answer to this desire. It is plain and simple.

LOVE

LOVE... THE KINGDOM... TRUTH... REAL WORLD...

YOU...

These are all one, all the same.

Did you hear me?

You are truth...

You are the kingdom...

You are the real world...

You are love.

You carry this knowingness deep within you.

If you allow yourself a moment to take that within you, you will know it is true!

What would keep you, then, from knowing this to be true but your perceptions of what you think you see; your perceptions taught to you by this insane world you think you have apparently just dropped into by accident...

Yet, has not the "world" of separation taught you that you are not what you truly are? Of course it has, for this world is the exact opposite of the kingdom. That is why I call this world unreal. It is because all that you see unlike love is illusion.

Your thoughts... any thought you have... creates its own apparent reality. For example, one might gaze their eyes upon this one known as Sadaam (or Osama Ben Laden, or Hitler). One might see this man as horrid, murderous, the worst of the worst, and the king of all darkness.

Yet, I say unto you, since thoughts create reality,

did not thoughts (murderous thoughts) have to be played out somewhere?

Have you not all had murderous thoughts? For, every thought creates its own world.

Thoughts that are out of alignment, such as

Judgment...

Hate...

Lack...

Guilt...

Shame...

all create a world of their own.

Many of these apparent realities have innocent souls that, out of love, play them out here in your illusion. That is why I say all are innocent! For all ones are but a reflection of your thoughts

LOVE is in alignment.

LOVE is the only truth.

Thoughts of anything other than LOVE seemingly are played out in your outer world. Those souls that come to do that dance for you are in service to the ONE! Yes, every soul here is in service to the ONE… here for the awakening of your mind; ONE MIND in service to itself.

How long would you have these innocent souls keep playing out your thoughts? I make no judgment here. Just asking!

Free will, my loves, free will!
When enough of you change your thoughts, those very souls will no longer have to come and play out your out of alignment illusions. Peace will be on your planet. Love will be all that you see.

You are a powerful creator.

You are ONE WITH ME.

Does that not speak of power?

Your thoughts are your prison, and yet in truth, they are your way home.

Love is your reality. All that you see is innocent. And since all minds are ONE, when you change your thoughts and see all as perfect you are changing apparent reality and opening a space for all souls to experience the truth of themselves.

This is why we have always said "The answers to your earth's problems begin within yourself." When you come to realize the POWER that lives within you (you and I as one), you will then assume responsibility for your thoughts. And when you do assume this responsibility you are Christ incarnate. You are doing the deepest, most honorable service any soul can bring to this planet.

You create much greater changes than going out and feeding a million children. For feeding the children is honorable and good, yet the problem — the underlying reality of thought that creates these worlds of lack and sorrow, cannot be healed until we change our thoughts and heal them within.

ONE MIND!

LOVE HEALS ALL THINGS!

LOVE EMBRACES ALL THINGS!

LOVE IS THE ANSWER TO ALL OF

THE WORLD'S PROBLEMS!

Let your "new" eyes be born in love and brought forth. See all things as innocent and free. Let love become your food for the day. Let love be your passion for each moment.

Let love be your very reason for existence. For, in truth, it is why you exist. LOVE birthed you; this is plain and simple!

30 days… SEE ONLY LOVE! BE ONLY LOVE!

Jeshua thru denisa

LESSON NINE

The only reality there is, is experienced in the NOW. Our purpose in this world of duality is to bring everything into our NOW for enjoyment and healing. In the NOW, a spirit of allowing all, forgiving all, and surrendering all to the source of Love brings us to the peace and joy of living that we truly desire.

LIVING IN THE NOW

The NOW, my sweet souls, is where I, the Space for Love, abide. I do not abide in the past. I do not abide in the future. All that is real is NOW, and the only reality is love.

Pay attention to creation. Look around you. Do not all things birthed in "time" end in "time? Do you ever see one creation that does arise in time not pass away in time? Yet, in truth, in the real world all lives all-ways.

Consciousness of your very life… your very passion for living… is only alive in and within your NOW moments.

Learn to see your past with your new eyes. Allow your past to become your NOW, because when unwanted memories appear in your consciousness NOW they can be changed, and only in the NOW can loving memories be enjoyed.

All can only be NOW!

All can only be alive NOW!

All can only be experienced NOW!

So, allow your past when it comes into your beautiful mind to be what it is.

If it is a glorious loving thought, feel the love.

If it is a painful memory, it is only there NOW for one purpose: to be healed.

And how would you heal that seeming memory which, in truth, is alive NOW because you are "feeling it now?"

Embrace that painful memory, and ask to see it with new eyes.

Ask ME, the Source of Love, to join with you in the healing of this memory.

What would I do with this memory but ask you to bring that painful memory down into your heart center?

There in that heart center is where all true power resides.

There is where I abide with YOU. Bring it down into your heart, place it in my hands, the hands of extended Love. Ask to see things differently.

Then

ALLOW!

ALLOW!

ALLOW!

You will come to know how this memory can be healed by giving it to me, by surrendering that person, place or thing to the Love that we are together there in your heart center, not the physical heart, but our sacred heart beating as One. That very process will heal all past painful memories.

The Voice for Love will bring into your outer world everything you need to "see" as the true perception of the event.

This true perception is allowed so you can heal the memory.

This true perception is allowed so you can transcend it, and take it back to the light.

It will be as if that Voice for Love came along with a broom and swept it from your mind.

You will come to see that the "power" it had over you will just slip away back to where it came from, which is unreality.

Let your past become your greatest tool. Let the loving memories flow through you like the cooling wind on a warm day.

Fill yourself with that love, for it is in your NOW, and it is good!

Allow your painful, hurtful past to come up as well, for it surely will.

Embrace it… Allow it…

Surrender it to the Voice for Love, and forgive it…

Forgive the one in front of you, and forgive yourself for all unreality you came to "see" about it. For in truth, all is innocent and free.

Nothing happens by chance; there are no accidents in this glorious universe. Know your NOW as your way home. Look *around you. What do you see in your NOW that seems to be unlike love?*

Allow yourself to admit that what you have in life you have truly desired.

Allow all of these: your desires, dreams and passion.

Block no feeling, no emotion.

Judge not any of these.

I Am there always in your NOW, and I AM but Love.

You will find me no where else but in your NOW. For, in truth, all has always only been NOW.
You are infinite, eternal glorious beings, and you are always creating new NOWS.

Your very life is the process by which you receive love, extend love and experience the results of that love.

YOU, only you, are my communication devices.

You are an extension of all that is LOVE.

In this world, you are here to live, enjoy and be the presence of LOVE.

The more you live in the now, and allow all that is in the now to be seen, owned, transmuted or enjoyed, the more you clear up your energy fields.

Thereby, more of what we are together, Love in Form, can be extended outward.

That is your only purpose: to be the extension of LOVE.

Let your NOW become your path to life, love and all that is.

Owning what you see and celebrating it is your pathway HOME.

So, thirty days, my sweet souls, live in the NOW as often as you think of it, and you will see the gifts that are always being brought unto you in every moment. These gifts are always there for you in the symbols of your NOW moments.

Peace be with you always,

The Voice and Source for Love,

Jeshua thru denisa

LESSON TEN

In lesson two, the message was about how our desires bring forth our experiences. In Lesson Ten, the message is about choice and how we come to experience the peace of God through conscious choice. All anxiety stemming from thoughts of threats to survival and safety, illness, scarcity and the like disappear when we consciously choose peace.

PEACE

There is a feeling of peace that passes all understanding. It comes from the knowingness that all is well; that all is in divine order.

But mostly, it arrives when you choose for it.

Yes, my sweet souls, you are the creator.

When you make a conscious choice for peace, your soul sends out a call to all of creation.

Creation stands there always in its neutrality. Your wish is its command.

When you choose peace, your "field of peace" is activated.

The Call has been heard.

Creation is alive with joy, and it brings to you all that you have "created" in your present NOW that is unlike peace for you to see.

For, in truth, you cannot create peace in your life if you do not "see" how you have created everything unlike it.

So, there is a process; I will call it the "undoing."

And yes, for a while you may feel a little "undone," so to say. And yet, in that glorious moment that you choose peace your peace is assured!

It can't help but be, for you are the creator and you have chosen.

Peace is a vibration.

It is knowingness.

When you begin your journey back to your true state, PEACE, everything, everything unlike it shows up.

It becomes a wow moment; you will need to hold onto the rails of trust.

This trusting in itself is the first step.

The letting go of all that you have created is the next.

You, my sweet souls, have been practicing surrender now, and it will be necessary for this walk of your sojourn.

Let go of all that is "shown" to you that is unlike peace. Be willing to walk through your rings of fear and doubt.

You may say, "How can I let go of this friend, this relationship, this job, and so on and so on?"

I say unto you, my beloved friend, this is your "WAY HOME TO PEACE."

You will need to trust that river of love that is flowing within you always. Be willing to place your wholeness into the middle of the river.

Let go of all that is hanging out along the sides of the river that feels unlike peace, for those very things are the "rings" your own soul has brought to you to guide you home.

This is your journey, and it was designed by you before you chose to come home to LOVE.

All souls will pass through this eye of the needle in order to come home to their

ONENESS

TOTALITY

FULL SELF

LOVE

ALL THAT IS.

Every soul is free to choose when, but all must choose this journey at some time to come home.

You are free to choose another time and another place, but the same "road" will have to be walked at some point in your human life.

And so, my sweet souls, why not NOW? What better time than NOW? Your journey into shadow has brought you much pain and suffering.

These tools I would give you in this NOW moment are the keys to your true life. They are your way home to LOVE.

I HAVE BEEN WAITING FOR SO LONG

FOR THESE WORDS TO FILL YOU

AND FOR YOU TO HEAR MY CALL

FOR IN TRUTH, IT IS YOUR CALL.

YES, DEAR ONES, YOU HAVE BEEN CALLING

FROM THE DEPTHS OF YOUR BEING-NESS FOR A VERY LONG "TIME."

Allow yourself to take a moment.

Breathe in the love that exists in the very air you breathe.

When you breathe in, you take in the love of the unformed.

When you breathe out, you breathe out that unformed and bring it into form. Breathe in that unformed love that is waiting for you every moment.

NOW, take it deep within your belly.

Then, breathe out the thought of Peace. Literally, feel the breath of peace flowing out of your mouth, knowing it will form in your world.

Do this whenever the inclination comes to you.

There is a vibration.

Feel the vibration of home.

These words are merely the vibration of home.

The words themselves are symbols, but the vibration behind them is calling to your soul. If you feel this NOW, it is your TIME.

ONLY LOVE EXISTS, MY DEAR SOULS.

Choose peace.

Choose peace for 30 days,

Want it, desire it, think it and be it always and in all-ways. And after a short time of undoing all unlike it, you will come to know that

NEVER, EVER IN REALITY

HAS ANYTHING ELSE

EVER TRULY EXISTED.

I AM just undoing your illusions, my heart of hearts.

Peace be with you always,

The Voice for Love,

The Voice for Peace,

The Holy Voice within us all,

Jeshua thru denisa

LESSON ELEVEN

Gratitude is based on allowing and trusting that all is unfolding for the benefit of your Fullest Self. This is the Self that was created as the Son of the Father Creator to share in the full life of the Father. An attitude of gratitude supports the bridge that takes your small self back to the consciousness of this Fullness.

GRATITUDE

Oh, yes my sweet ones,
Another way to express this thought
Is GREAT ATTITUDE OF TRUST.

Gratitude is what you must cultivate
As you choose your souls journey home.
The choice has been made,
The end is certain,
And of that, you must TRUST.

As you cultivate the seed of
TRUST

YOU WILL COME TO KNOW

THAT EVERY MOMENT IS ONE

TO BE GRATEFUL FOR,
For all your NOW Moments
Are coming directly from
Your Highest
SELF.

They are being delivered to you
Like dinner at your finest restaurant.
Every moment is to be cherished,
Allowed,
And it IS for YOU to know
That it is miraculous…
It is LOVE itself that now
Lives your life…

Gratitude is another way of
Saying to this unseen ONE
THAT ALL IS WELL,
NO MATTER HOW IT APPEARS…
It is acknowledging that
Every moment you are now experiencing
Will be allowed,
Because you KNOW IT IS YOUR WAY
HOME TO LOVE;
YOUR VERY NATURE…

Gratitude needs to be cultivated.
It is a seed that brings
The most beautiful flowers
Of your very self
Into full bloom…

You may be looking at your driveway,
That at this very Now Moment,
Seems to have NO Car to get into…
How did that happen??
Why is this so??
Gratitude my sweet ones…
Just say, I don't know why this is so,
But I am grateful for it.
It is my way home,
And I TRUST AND KNOW
THAT ALL IS WELL,
Therefore, I am grateful for it…

This GREAT ATTIDUDE
WILL BRING YOU GIFTS
Beyond your earthly ideas of gifting…
For the gifts I bring to you
Are not of this world

They are that of the Real World…
And I promise you
They will show themselves
To YOU…

Be grateful for all that you see.
Know that it is the bridge home
That was created in the very moment
You had a thought
Of creating separate from the
ONE.

Nurture your seed of gratitude.
Water it with the thoughts of trust.
Feed it with the mind of KNOWING.
When you notice it starting to bloom
Look at it with loving eyes…
Those eyes are the very windows of
your soul
And they are saying to you
ALL IS GOOD…
I am loved beyond measure
I AM HERE FOR A PURPOSE…

I AM LOVED,
I AM LOVING,
I AM LOVABLE
FOREVER!!!!!

I am that ONE
Birthed before the thought
Of time and space...
I am the sky.
I am the stars in the sky.
I am the very breath that I breathe
I am all of it!!!

Of that, my sweet souls
You can be certain.
For it has always been
SO!!!!

THIRTY DAYS
CHOOSE GRATITUDE

And then allow and trust

PEACE BE WITH YOU ALWAYS

THE VOICE FOR LOVE

Jeshua thru denisa

LESSON TWELVE

Let the real you, your passionate Self, touch every aspect of your life in this world of duality that attempts to hide your true nature. Be aware of what brings you joy. Notice and welcome your feelings of passion. Follow your bliss and take every thing you have and go with you for the ride.

PASSION

Passion, my sweet souls of ONE LIGHT DIVINE, is your inheritance.

It is, in truth, who you are.

It is that passion that you feel in fleeting moments in time that is your soul's calling to you.

Your passion, and the "feeling" of it, is what created you.

Passion is what brought you into form.

Passion, the very presence of it, creates mansions in the house of the ONE, the only begotten Child of the Creator God.

The energy of passion ignites your being-ness...

your consciousness in love.

Feeling "passion" is when you will most remember your true nature.

That feeling of "passion" is, in truth, who you are.

You are Passion. You are the thought of it; you are the result of it.

YOU ARE IT!

Please take a moment to take that within you, for, if you truly live with "passion," all the closed doors to your true nature will burst open like the sun bursts upon the earth in its every waking moment.

In every moment it shines, the sun embraces and warms all it envelops.

You are the spirit's rays that are always one with the sun we call "passion." Passion envelops you like the ocean tenderly touches the sand.

Passion is

YOUR RIGHT.

IT IS YOUR LIFE.

PASSION IS YOUR VERY BEING-NESS.

Ignite it, sweet ones. Follow it. Let all that you do be created with it.

Be it!

Feel it!

Own it!

Then, live it!

Live your passion full out.

Let all those worries of what could, would, should happen if you dared to live with passion go.

Give all those worries to me, for they are based on an illusion that keeps you in a box of struggle.

You were not birthed for struggle.

You were birthed to create from your passion.

You have practiced allowance.

You have practiced surrender.

You have learned of desire.

You have nurtured gratitude.

Take all of those new flowers you have been blooming these last few lessons and now:

Follow your passion!

Follow your bliss!

Your very sacred heart IS passion.

Notice NOW, each day, that which brings you a momentary feeling of passion, of bliss, of joy. PAY ATTENTION.

You will then come to see all that you are doing without passion.

NOW, you can bring passion even to those very every day moments which seem to be apart from your bliss.

You can say out loud:

I AM ALIVE.

I AM ONE WITH GOD.

I AM WASHING THIS DISH,

AND IT IS GOOD.

PASSION!

BLISSFULNESS!

JOYFULNESS!

Sweet souls, passion is a glorious thought; an en-lightened experience of life.

So, thirty days

Follow your passion and enjoy it. Sit in your bliss! Bring your passion to all! You are loved beyond measure. Know this as your closest truth.

I love you so,

The Voice for Love!

The Voice for Joy!

The Voice for Bliss!

The Voice of Passion!

The Voice you are and were created to be always and for all time!

Jeshua thru denisa

LESSON THIRTEEN

Jeshua here makes the distinction between happiness and joy. He does not deprecate happiness or any emotion or feeling but asks us to notice the temporary nature of all our feelings. Joy, on the other hand is a permanent state of well-being arising out of a knowingness of who we are.

JOY

Joy has been very misunderstood on your earth plane.

It very often is confused with happiness.

They are two very, very different things in your life.

Happiness is fleeting.

It is a feeling, like all others that have been "birthed" in time.

And time, my friends, is an illusion.

Happiness arises and passes away like all other feelings birthed in time. Happiness comes, and it goes.

It is temporal. (Temporary)

It is to be enjoyed in the moment.

Happiness is of God, as all feelings are.

Feelings of sadness arise and pass away, as they are also temporal.

Anything in your world that arises and passes away is not true JOY!

So, allow your moments of happiness, and also, allow your moments of sadness, for all have a purpose.

It is those ones who strive to always feel that temporal happiness that become addicted to substances that can only bring temporary moments of happiness; of pleasure...

They think they have experienced a feeling of home (a sense of heaven) and continue to try and duplicate it through alcohol, drugs, food, sex, competition, exercise and the like.

When you live in Joy...

when you know you are a being who exists in JOY, addictions will fall away like the clothes outgrown.

They will just simply be of no use, for they serve no purpose.

When LIGHT (consciousness of who you are as Love) enters your life, joy becomes your "Knowingness."

You will know those other moments only bring something temporary, and the love that you are re-membering will simply dissolve those choices, sending them back to where they came from, which is NO-WHERE!

So, what is joy?

IT IS KNOWINGNESS.

IT IS ETERNAL.

IT IS YOUR TRUE STATE OF BEING.

Joy is the gift given unto you.

It is the life of your very life.

For, in truth, your body, your earth space suit, while on the earth plane cannot be anywhere that love is not.

You are so enveloped in LOVE that you are always swimming in the seamless sea of loving synchronicity.

In every moment, it is as if you are the wave of the ocean.

Each wave is still one with the ocean.

Each wave is unique, yet still One with the ONE.

If you could wrap your thoughts around it, you would know You are the Ocean.

You are the Wave.

You are all of it.

You are like the dew drop is to the ocean that receives it always and in all ways.

THIS KNOWINGNESS IS YOUR TRUE STATE.

IT IS JOY.

When you live from this knowingness that you are pure love...

pure divine light...

when you practice all these lessons which will undo your small ego…

the one that has taught you fear, shame and guilt, you will come to know the

JOY of LIFE.

You will come to know that all that has ever existed within your earth body has always been DIVINE LOVE.

It has been your small ego, that voice you listen to, that has taught you to buy into guilt, shame and fear.

As those ego thoughts, that have created what you think is your reality, are laid aside. like toys you have outgrown, you will SEE YOURSELF

IN ALL OF YOUR GRANDNESS,

IN ALL OF YOUR DIVINITY,

IN ALL OF YOUR TRUTH.

You are one with me ALWAYS.

THAT IS JOY! THAT IS GOOD!

SO, my sweet ones,

30 days

Feel the knowingness of JOY that you are

ONE WITH LOVE ALWAYS.

It could never not be so.

30 days

Joy, joy, joy.

Peace be with you always. You abide in JOY forever.

The Voice for Love,

Jeshua thru denisa

LESSON FOURTEEN

Knowingness is living in heaven while still experiencing the world of duality. Each of us, as we awaken to the truth of our identity, is the light that shines upon the world of duality and reveals to all, who have eyes to see and ears to hear, the truth of their identity as the One creation of the One Creator God.

KNOWINGNESS

Ah, my sweet ones, knowingness is the fruit of the fruit.

It is the life of your very life. It is the joy of your joy.

*Knowingness is a state of being-ness, and it is HOME.
When you live from KNOWINGNESS, YOU ARE HOME!*

Yes, my sweet hearts, you can be home while on earth. That is where this very world you see is headed.

The light of the ONE is descending on your planet. It is dispelling all unlike it, and it is YOU who are choosing for it, that are "descending" it right into your very self...your human body.

You are birthing Christ Mind on earth.

You are the SECOND COMING, AND YOU ARE BEAUTIFUL

TO SEE.

When you live in "Knowingness," there is only peace.

Nothing, no-thing you see with your earthly eyes is unacceptable to you. You are healed. You are One with All.

You KNOW FROM THE DEPTHS OF YOUR BEING

THAT ALL THINGS ARE PERFECTLY PERFECT,

in perfect mo-tion, for the journey home...

All is allowed... All is seen as good...

Trust has become your sword of truth...

Allowance has become the very substance of your life...

Gratitude for all has now found a home in your mind...

Praise for all of creation, exactly as it appears, is your new way of living, for you now KNOW that all that you are seeing is the bridge home.

This bridge has always been here, but it has been clouded by the thoughts of fear, lack, guilt and shame.

Those very things are illusions to you now.

You have set them aside, and you now walk on the very road that I walked on seemingly before you, and even that is a bit of an illusion, For all IS NOW!

Ponder that statement, my sweet ones.

ALL IS NOW!

So, while you live in your "Knowingness," you have become a vehicle for the extension of LOVE.

You "KNOW" your only purpose "Now" is to extend love, to allow that love that lives within to run your show.

You ask of that voice always "what would you have me do?"

That voice is your new employer.

You have no "other" job, for the false self, the personality self, has fallen away.

All that is left is a vehicle to express the LOVE that you are, your highest self,

GOD,

ABBA,

ALL THAT IS,

HAS COME HOME.

It is the driver of your car, the gas in your engine, the rose in your garden.

You are now living life here on planet earth IN THE ETERNAL NOW OF HOME.

Wake up on your next morning, and say out loud,

"I AM THAT ONE.

I AM CHRIST.

I AM THE LIVING FRUIT OF THE THOUGHT OF LOVE,

AND I AM GOING TO LIVE IT FULL STEAM,

AND THAT VOICE FOR LOVE IS GOING TO DRIVE ME EVERYWHERE I NEED TO GO,

AND, IT IS GOING TO SPEAK TO ME IN EVERY MO-MENT SO THAT I CAN ONLY BE THE EXTENSION OF THAT BEAUTY BY THE GIFT OF GRACE IN THIS WORLD."

What other purpose could there possibly be in life?

What grander way of living could ever be experienced?

30 days, my sweet ones

30 days of KNOWINGNESS

Peace be with you always,

THE VOICE FOR LOVE,

Jeshua thru denisa

LESSON FIFTEEN

Our only reality is that all things, all wishes, all that is, is ours through the grace of our Creator. Always was this so, but we choose to see things through a darkened glass of duality and separation. Our willingness to release these false perceptions back to the void of nothingness from which they came allows the total, unconditional grace of God to again be clear to our restored vision of reality.

GRACE AS REALITY

You have been birthed into a world of time by your own choice.

You have come to this planet, at this particular time, for a purpose.

There are no accidents in this world.

There is never, never a moment in time that you are not right where you are supposed to be always.

IN TRUTH, LIFE IS LIVING YOU.

Look around you, my sweet souls, look at all that you see with new eyes, for all that you see, all that you could see in any moment of your time is showing you that everything is "separate."

It is showing you that you are separate from your brother and sister.

After all, I see that one next to me, and that one could not be me.

The trees, birds, animals are all separate from me.

I could go on and on, and yet, my sweet souls, you are living in an illusion, an illusion of being separate.

I tell you NOW, THERE IS ONLY ONE BEING HERE. YES, ONLY ONE

APPEARING SEPARATE.

You are that ONE, your brother and your sister are that ONE. Your perceptions of what you see are what keep you in duality.

These days are coming to a close.

I came here to your earth and walked this plane.

I felt all the emotions, pain, joy, and all the rest that you experience daily, and I came to see through a change in perception that only

LOVE IS REAL.

Grace is that Reality.

It is the only true Reality, and all of you,

ALL OF YOU ONLY LIVE IN THAT REALITY, IN TRUTH.

What keeps you from seeing that this is true is your perceptions.

*The undoing of the mind, the "small ego," is what is
necessary to see only heaven,
only love.*

The small ego keeps you in bondage.

It has taught you that you are not ONE.

*It has fooled you into believing that the one in front
of you is not YOU.*

However, I say unto you, there is no one here but you.

There is no-thing here but you.

ALL IS YOU.

ALL IS GOD.

All IS ABBA,

And you are that.

And I repeat:

GRACE IS OUR REALITY,

*AND THE ONLY THING THAT KEEPS YOU FROM SEEING
ONLY GRACE*

IS YOUR PERCEPTIONS.

*Everything you see is God, in density, and because there is no-
thing here that is not GOD, you are bathed in love's presence.*

You are NEVER not within the loving arms of love except within your THOUGHTS!

When you change your thoughts, your perceptions of what you think you see, when you allow, surrender and choose to see only love, you will come to know that there is only Heaven.

I am the VOICE FOR LOVE.

I LIVE WITHIN EACH OF YOU

ALWAYS,

AND WITHIN MY HEART, THAT I SHARE WITH YOU, IF YOU WOULD BUT MEET ME THERE, WE WILL UNDO YOUR PERCEPTIONS THAT HAVE HELD YOU IN DUALITY.

If you have reached this lesson and practiced the previous lessons, you have begun to undo what you thought this world was for.

You believe you are a body. You believe that what you see in front of you is solid, and I say to you none of it is real.

Even the body is an illusion.

Now, where did this body come from?

It came from within your HOLY MIND.

Yes, you, the creator, have birthed a body from within your mind, your soul.

In truth, there is nothing outside of YOU.

ALL IS WITHIN YOU.

You ARE GRAND, GLORIOUS,

ETERNAL.

YOU ARE ONE WITH GOD, ALWAYS.

So, Grace, Grace is your reality.

The ego has taught you that you could be guilty, you could be fearful, and that shame is acceptable, but I say unto you, when you undo your perceptions, when you come to me in your Heart center, when you bring all things to me to be made right, which is just right mindedness, you will come to see that you could never be anything but innocence.

This undoing of the mind is necessary, and it begins with admitting

I DO NOT KNOW WHAT A SINGLE THING

IS OR WHAT IT IS FOR!

It is in your admitting that you know NOTHING and that this ONE within me DOES that you WILL COME TO THIS VOICE for Love within,

AND SURRENDER.

You will ask this voice for love, "What is this for?"

That practice WILL TAKE YOU TO HEAVEN.

I WILL COME TO YOU.

I may whisper gently in your ear or show you pictures in your mind, but I WILL COME.

ALL YOU NEED TO DO IS OPEN THE DOOR TO YOUR HEART.

Grace as reality. Grace is your inheritance. Grace will "descend" upon you whenever you let go.

Hold my hand, and let me gently remove all the cob webs from your heart. Let me clear out all the thoughts that keep you from

KNOWING YOU ARE ONE WITH GOD AND THAT YOU ARE THAT!

Grace is the love of the ONE descended into your heart center that brings you back to right mindedness. Grace descends and en-lightens your being-ness.

So, for the next thirty days, my sweet ones, remember you live in Grace.

Wake up each morning and say out loud,

"I CHOOSE LOVE. ONLY LOVE IS REAL, AND IF I SEE ANYTHING THIS DAY THAT APPEARS UNLIKE IT, I WILL COME TO THAT ONE IN MY HEART FOR RIGHT PERCEPTION."

CAN YOU DO THIS FOR ME?

What gifts wait for you, my sweet souls.

I love you. All of creation loves you. Come to me now.

GRACE AS REALITY IS THE ONLY TRUE REALITY. GRACE IS THE ONLY THING THAT EXISTS ETERNALLY.

Only truth exists. It is timeless.

Anything that is of time is an illusion, my sweet ones. Come home to your reality now.

The voice for love,

Jeshua thru denisa

LESSON SIXTEEN

The chatter in our mind is like the static heard when many radio stations compete for our attention. Allowing silence to replace all these stations allows the One real station to speak to us of our truth as the child of our One Creator. Awareness of this truth gives us access to all knowledge. This knowledge allows us to embrace all in its neutrality and to allow the love that created all to become manifest to us in all.

SILENCE, THE GATEWAY TO YOUR HOLY MIND

You have heard many times the kingdom is within.

There has never in 'time" been anything said that is more of truth than this:

THE KINDGOM IS WITHIN.

And what is this kingdom?

It is true knowledge.

It is that which lays aside the small ego, literally flattens it into dust.

It is that which restores, en-lightens, brings truth, brings ever more love, and ever more peace to your soul.

"The Kingdom Within" is that which has ALL KNOWLEDGE, AND IT LIVES WITHIN YOUR HOLY MIND.

It lives within you, always.

So, that said, "Silence," silence is that stillness, it is that space, it is the "way" for the Voice for Love to whisper into your Heart.

Silence is also the willingness to leave the distractions of this world, to leave them behind, for just a moment, and hear The VOICE FOR LOVE.

Silence is that place where miracles abide and where your true nature is realized by Your Self.

In the beginning, this silence needs to be cultivated.

It needs to be visited.

It needs to be honored.

It needs to be invited.

Then, as you create a space of silence, more and more you will come to hear

The VOICE FOR LOVE.

It may come as a gentle wind across your hair, a gentle touch upon your neck. Silence may speak in your heart and answer your questions.

Whatever is necessary for you to feel the presence of love, you will find in the spaciousness of Silence.

It is YOUR WAY TO ME.

That said, it also is a place of deep honesty.

Silence is the willingness to "look" at "your" creations honestly, for we cannot transcend that which we do not embrace.

Only by embracing, do we give all of our creations the gift of innocence.

We literally bring them back to their neutrality, and then, the love of the comforter can come in and heal it, can restore it, can uplift, literally lifting it from your heart.

This is a true CREATIVE PROCESS,

AND IT SETS YOU FREE.

The ONE in front of you is your savior.

The ONE in front of you is Christ in body.

It serves you by reflecting to you that which is not healed within yourself.

If you have a "reaction" to something someone says or does,

IT IS YOURS, ALWAYS.

Trust me, that this is so.

Once you have stated to the ONE that you want to bring your soul home, all of creation comes to you to answer your call.

An example:

A woman pulls up next to you in your little vehicles you would call a car. She screams at you for not turning on your blinker. (Oh, heaven forbid!) So, she is screaming her head off at you now. NOW, you step back and you take a breath. Wow, how did I create this moment in my life today? I do not like this moment.

"SHE IS A Jerk!" On and on with your head, you continue. "Gee, I am glad I am not her!" So on and so on.

This, THIS IS YOUR SMALL EGO.

It is telling you that something, anything you see, exists OUTSIDE OF YOURSELF.

I TELL YOU IT DOES NOT.

So, what is this for?

Here is your way home, come to me, sweet one, ask of me

"What is this for?"

Take a moment and create a gentle spaciousness, silence, for me to come and answer.

Now, in truth, this ONE IS SCREAMING AT YOU TO LOOK AT WHERE YOUR FEELINGS OF ANGER ARE UNHEALED.

Something within you that wants to be released and that will come to you from the voice for love...

This is a personal journey for each.

So, I hope I am undoing your illusion that anything, anyone exists outside of YOU. That is untrue.

It is the ego mind wanting to keep you in separateness to survive, and we are squashing it like a gnat.

So, my beautiful ones, and you are truly beautiful, we are undoing the dream, we are in the process of bringing heaven to earth for, in truth, it has always been here except for the thoughts in your mind that have brought about what you would perceive to be eons and eons of wars, lack, and all the rest.

And this, because of a single thought, where you forgot to laugh, for you see

Seriousness,

Seriousness

keeps things in place.

Laughter uplifts. Laughter, breaks up the energy.

SO, SILENCE. I LIVE WITHIN YOUR SILENCE.

I LIVE WITHIN YOUR HEART CENTER.

I LIVE WITHIN YOU ALWAYS.

I LOVE YOU.

How could it not be so?

If you could see your true self as I do, you would know why I love you.

For, when I see you, I honor the creator's choice.

There is no grander love than yourself.

Find that within, so that you may be my hands and my feet as we undo your ego mind. It makes room for you to transform your body mind into a clear vehicle from which only love can be extended into the world.

What grander purpose in life could there ever be?

So, Silence.

Practice silence deeply, for your next 30 days.

Continue to allow, surrender,

desire, and KNOW
that only Love is Real.

Peace be with you always.

The Voice for Love,

Jeshua thru denisa

LESSON SEVENTEEN

Allowing all without judgment of any person and event brings all to neutrality. Duality, formed by the perception of separateness, can no longer remain a solid perception in a state of neutrality. Without duality, all is free to be what it is created to be, an expression of loving peacefulness eternally. You need do nothing to achieve this state of peace eternal but to allow all to be without e-motional reaction. And if there is e-motional reaction that is to be allowed as well.

ALLOWANCE

Denise just said to me...

We already did a lesson on allowance.

She hesitated; she resisted this lesson, for in her Holy Mind she thought this Voice was making a mistake, not hearing me correctly...

Well, she is not hearing me in error.

We are coming around to allowance one more time...

Over these last few months, we have been undoing much from your mind...

You may have even begun to see the innocent dance this is behind all of creation, the bleeding "in," so to say, of that which your earthly eyes cannot quite grasp.

So, allowance.

I am going to go deeper into this now for a purpose.

For the next 30 days, diligently allow in every moment all things.

That could be your car breaks down.

It could be your job is gone.

Whatever it is does not matter.

Just allow it. Be with it. Trust it.

Know that YOU do NOT know what a single thing is or what it is for...

When you do this simple task and you pay attention, you will see that all things that happen, in your every moment, are a gift to you, always a gift no matter how it appears.

And why would I say this?

Because only LOVE IS REAL, AND THERE IS NO OTHER WAY FOR YOU TO BECOME AWARE OF THIS FACT THAN TO ALLOW ALL THINGS.

In that allowance, you will come to see that even that which appears unlike love, in truth, IS LOVE, a GIFT TO YOU FROM SPIRIT.

This, my sweet souls, takes much diligence.

It also takes much trust that the words I am sharing here are the truth.

By now, you have come to literally feel the vibration behind these words.

As you read these words and try to take them in Love, Love's vibration is what is calling you.

It exists behind the words, for the words are merely symbols.

It is the vibration behind these words that are truly speaking to your soul, your true self, and deep within you somewhere by now you KNOW THIS IS TRUE.

So, allow,

Allow.

Allow the vibrations to touch you.

Allow the thoughts to come to the mind.

Allow the gentle dance that has been prepared for you by your higher Self, who is Now running the show to teach you anew.

For, if you are reading these words, and you have come upon this lesson 17, you have already decided to allow Love to guide you home to your true Reality while still living in duality on earth.

Duality, my sweet souls is slipping away, and it is good!

It is literally being dissolved by all the YOU's that are seeing all events as neutral…

that are allowing, in time, the illusion to be what it is…

that are giving not ONE MORE MOMENT of their holy thought to anything that appears unlike love, for, by the seeing of neutrality…

by seeing that all things, no matter how they appear are the bridge home...

by coming within to your voice for love, you and you alone are literally the savior of the world.

For, you see you have changed your HOLY MIND, and what the SON DECREES IS!

So, another 30 days of diligent allowance.

Some fear may come up, some feelings of loss may come up, and it is okay.

Allow it.

All that is not in vibration with YOUR Soul will want to leave because it no longer can exist, for only creations of matching vibration can truly exist in the same space.

So, all that needs to go, will go, and it is a blessing.

It is literally going to bring you in the end Heaven to your heart, Love to your soul, the golden era, peace on earth,

And YOU are a part Of THAT.

WHAT A GREAT PURPOSE YOU HAVE.

I LOVE YOU.

It could not be different, for, in truth, You and I are ONE.

We exist together always in the real world, that which is still a bit unseen to you.

Yet, only that LOVE will exist upon your earth soon!

And that is a promise.

A promise kept from a very seemingly distant time, and yet, all is NOW.

So, another 30 days… Allowance.

You are sooooo loved,

The Voice for Love,

Jeshua thru denisa

LESSON EIGHTTEEN

The one who seems to be apart from you and in opposition to you and your wants and wishes is but you showing yourself the hidden corners of your soul that you have denied. They are, thereby, revealing all the things that represent the "not you;" all the things you have stuffed in the closets of your mind. A willingness to forgive allows your "Fuller Self" to scrub these closets clean, so that, the true "Light of the World" you are, can shine brightly for all to see.

WHY FORGIVENESS?

You have heard spoken many times the importance of forgiveness, yet, humanity has not understood the symbol (forgiveness), nor the true meaning of "do unto others."

In its simplest form, forgiveness of another is forgiveness of your own soul.

All are YOU, my sweet ones, you can not possibly lay your beautiful eyes upon ONE thing in space and time that is not YOU.

You are all ONE thing, ONE beautiful truth, LIGHT....

YOUR BODIES ARE A COALESCENCE OF THOUGHT IN FORM.

You believe you are separate from the ONE across from you, yet, it is a wholly ONE Relationship.

When the ONE in front of you "ruffles your feathers," it is YOU, it is GOD in front of you showing you your edges that have not been healed...

In truth, it is a beautiful dance if ONE would allow it...

The ONE in front of you who you may think to be your enemy is, in truth, bringing you a grand gift, the gift of seeing your hidden thought patterns that are, in truth, clouding your view of Yourself as pure light!

Therefore, they are your savior. How else could it be, my sweet ones?

I have been saying that all Is GOD, that means ALL;

THE VERY AIR YOU BREATHE IS GOD.

ALL IS...

YOU ARE...

For you to re-member that this is so, that you are ONE with ME;

ABBA;

All that is,

YOU must release the ways of the small ego, for it is this belief in the small ego that has formed your reality.

Please, sweet ones, it is time, yes, it is time to CHANGE YOUR MINDS...

One thought away AM I from YOU and that thought is ONLY LOVE IS REAL. Change your minds, my sweet ones, I am right there with you, waiting.

I am soooooooooo much a part of YOU that there is no separation ever, there is no where you can look, see or perceive that is not of ME and the same is true of YOU.

You are walking with blinders on, it has always been so on your earth plane of illusion.

Wake up this today and claim

I AM ONE WITH GOD,

AND I AM GOING TO LET GO OF ALL THAT IS NOT OF LOVE…

If the one in front of me is reflecting anger I am going to KNOW that I have not healed my soul's own belief in separateness.

I am going to go within;

find my edges of anger;

forgive the one in front of me;

thank that one for reflecting it to me, and forgive myself.

That simple, my sweet ones, that simple!!!

In doing such grand inner work you raise your vibration,

and as you raise it more and more you come to see that THERE IS ONLY LIGHT.

You are literally transforming your body to light every time you release, for, it is only the creation of your "dark" thoughts that has kept you from ME.

The way is simple.

This is the time NOW, my sweet ones.

Can you imagine a NEW NOW where all you see, every moment in time

IS ABBA, IS GOD?

The more you let go of all thoughts that are unlike love, bring them to me to be transformed, the more you honor the Light that exists within ALL...

The more you love YOURSELF, KNOWING YOU ARE ONE WITH ME your loads will lighten, your heart will sing, and you will live in the vibration of pure love, and your planet will only reflect that you are the creators.

You have just been creating in error, come home to love, my sweet ones, I will meet you there!

So, thirty days, my sweet souls, retrain your holy mind to see the one in front of you IS YOU, AND THEY BRING THE GIFT of YOURSELF.

All of your past days of allowance, surrender, gratitude, and all the other lessons have brought you NOW to this point where you can truly see the gift in forgiveness, where NOW you will see the invisible dance of creation that some may call the "String" theory.

It is love in mo-tion.

It is the very means by which you will re-member who you truly are,

for, in truth, this whole series of lessons are only the road to awakening you to

WHO YOU TRULY ARE, LOVE; LIGHT;

it could never not be so!

Forgiveness will be the most important part of your sojourn with ME,
for, you are, in truth, forgiving your own soul for believing you could ever create separately from LOVE…

In the very depths of your being you want to wake up; re-member your true nature, and all of your planet, all of your universe, all that you see is in this process.

The Solar Flares that have been bombarding your planet are the very means by which the Creator is lighting up the world, changing the very meaning of your DNA.

Your bodies are changing, you are "heating" up, so to say, along with your planet, for you and mother earth are ONE, CONNECTED ALWAYS as one thing.

As you clear your energy field you raise your vibration and the planet's right along with it.

By doing these lessons you are bringing in HEAVEN TO EARTH AND TO ALL OF CREATION, ALL OF TIME AND SPACE.

That is how important this work is!

What grander purpose could any soul have?

If you are drawn to these words know that it is not an accident, there are no accidents in this world, for

I AM PERFECTION, AND SO ARE YOU, MY SWEET SOULS OF ONE LIGHT DIVINE.

Forgiveness diligently applied will bring you gifts never imagined, and this is a promise...

There is never a mo-ment in "time" that you are alone, my sweet souls.

Peace be with you always,

The voice for love,

Jeshua thru denisa

The messages of these 18 lessons is simple yet we avoid the simplicity in favor of drama and complexity. We came to this state of complex uncertainties for a reason. Our intent was to extend the truth of our being, as the Love created, even into the darkness of love denied. Now we return denied love to Self, the Source of Love.

In the extended lessons which follow, denisa, michael and anne joyfully commingle as an expression of returning this love to Source.

EXTENDED WRITINGS

Denisa/michael/anne/jeshua in these extended readings apply the lessons to their lives in the world of duality. Through their commingling they evidence the truth of these words. Although each of us is to seek the at-one-ment for ourselves much comfort and support is experienced as each compliments the other, holding hands as we walk across this Bridge to Home.

The Seed Within

After we exhaust enough drama and still find ourselves unfulfilled we turn within to find the seed of home. Tentatively, at first, but then with more and more trust in the beauty and truth of ourselves we allow this seed to burst forth

the seed within

we come in blind...at first, we only see the love of home
then, our earthly eyes open and we wonder what are we
doing here…

the curtain is pulled down, the light of home seems to have
taken flight

the heart takes on many wounds as we walk this life...

yet, there is a seed contained within us all already known in "heaven" when this seed cracks open...

as long as the world seems perfect the seed remains dormant for we are playing in the dream...

we get knocked down and yet we get back up again and look and look for the next perfect job, perfect mate, perfect book, etc....

one day we finally scream and say "this world cannot be real!"

ahhhhhhhhhh

the seed bursts open, we see the bridge already prepared for each of us that takes us back home to the truth of our self...

for some of us have created Jeshua, the name we give to the energies of transcendence that begin to burn away the illusion that we are this body, this little self...

the fires of transformation begin, we are the global warming

we are heating up of self, bringing up all unlike love so it can be returned to the beauty of love...

we are so loved by this gentle, loving comforter who comes along and wipes away

all that we are willing to let go of...

all beliefs outgrown...

all wounds are healed and we made new again, our hearts are opened and our I AM presence now has more space to descend into our earth body, lighting us up like a bright light not yet seen by this world....

now we are the walking light; we need not know how this light is blessing our world, the mystery of god continues to reveal itself; the symbols of love appear in the most wonderful of ways...

and now we know from the depths of our hearts we have never been alone....

we are loved beyond measure

denisa

from this seed within
the vastness of our being grows
to fill each nook and cranny
all darkness is enlightened
by our ever expanding willingness
to look and see our Self
in all that appears as "not me"

michael

the process

i came to you...

we tilled your garden...
together we pulled up the roots contained deep within
you that would flower —worlds of fear, lack, guilt and the
opposite of peace...

i put a protection of light around you as you walked
this path...

you learning to love you again...

i sent away many that would distract you from this journey;
for many of you much loss was felt... then, you woke up
and knew once again the love you are...

now, in that strength i will bring many back to you...
remember the term "turning the cheek?"

well, now that you stand in your knowingness of the love
you are you can witness the "world" anew by the turning
of your cheek, and seeing from the eye of love and peace...

you can bless all that you see, for, you now KNOW it as
illusion, now you stand with me and together we simply
bless the world for there is no "you" there any longer,
there is only

I AM

walk with me now and bless this world

jeshua thru denisa

EXPRESSING LOVE AND GRATITUDE

anne writes:

dearest michael,

"we" comes to mind...

a lovely word of commingling... a word that includes all inclusively

there is no one excluded

and in this "we" there are no mistakes...

perfect innocence abides and all that is encountered

is experience to embrace

and the "we" sees its' Self to be the extension of the

One

"we" swim in the sea of seamless, endless, love-filled synchronicity...

in the sea of the One

union, dear brother, we are participating in the allowing of union

to unfold on the planet

this union seeing with the eyes of Christ beholds love in every corner,

every relationship,

every interaction,

every thought,

every moment.

there is no-where that love is not

in full trust i sit with you; envisioning with you a new world

jeshua/anne

michael adds:

the circle of love grows ever wider and ever deeper

denisa continues:

i see the picture on the front of the book "the way of
the servant"

beautiful jeshua with his palms outstretched...

this is it

let us leave our palms in that outstretched position in all
moments

and continue to bless all that we see, for there is a
diamond

heart within each palm, and the power contained there

is not of this world.... this thought brings me much delight

love you both,

denisa

anne goes on singing of love commingling:

there is a swirling of heart energy around me this day.....
this hour.....this moment
there are names swirling in this tornado shaped energy
jeshua.....denisa.....michael.....
and now i can see my self with all of you
thank you, blessed beings of light who extend Love to me
in every moment
joy cannot be contained
this connection is the manifesting of a dream
where spirit collaboration
is recognized
and bodies, egos and personalities
are also recognized
as trappings to be released
as this new level of communication
takes flight
where trust is absolute
where love is known as who we are
i love you all in all ways,
anne

michael replies:

sooo sooo beautifully said

your heart is now bared of all encumbrances as is mine as
is denisa's
we join with jeshua as one and this has always been
our wish

more replies from anne:

dear michael,

you take my breath away!

what is there to say but.....

OH MY GOSH!!

YES!! I WOULD LOVE TO COLLABORATE.....

COORDINATE....

COOPERATE.....

COMMUNICATE....COMINNGLE...ETC.....ETC....

if i could think of any more words that begin with co.... i
would use them here!!

anne

michael responds:

my dearest anne,
i feel your presence with me as One. there is no
separation.
these powers all about us are awesomely formidable.

we are on the path of the servant of love and what a
delight to have such a lovely companion as you.

i love you sooo,
michael

to which denisa adds:

yes, we are so blessed to have each other...

you and anne bring such a sense of peace to my life...

yesterday i could feel the energies of transformation
of the whole

building intensely...

and then, i heard, the eye words.... (calmness in the eye of
the hurricane)

i sat down to write them and i absolutely knew that i am
the peace

within all things...

the knowingess is growing, and i know that our oneness
together

is our gift for this walk we have been willing to take...

the trust we have been willing to take within

and the love that we extend

i just keep remembering the sheep walking with the 2
babies, i would

not be surprised if one day soon i saw a 3rd

but it is always such a mystery....

i love you so, michael

for i am your heart, and you and anne are mine

denisa

merging of mind and heart

there is such a merging taking place.....
a joining of the seemingly separate
into the One Heart.
i feel the merging.
there is this sensation
that is without words.....
transitioning out of duality
as the mind and heart realize
Oneness
in all that is seen, felt, heard.
how extraordinary
to be witness....to be part of
this merging of self with Self.

anne

A LOVING GIFT I GAVE MYSELF

My son asked me to partake and join in a project for which I held no interest. My refusal brought sharp response of anger and attack. I pulled myself back and asked my guides "What is this for? What is he here to show me of the dark recesses of my mind?" Gracefully responses came:

"When time began you set upon a project you desired to initiate so you could feel alone and separate from me, your Source. You experienced unbearable pain. You cried to me to relieve you of this pain. As Source, I responded not, for Source could not enter into a dream of separation from itself." This provoked your cries, "Why are you allowing me to suffer so?.."

"Why are you abandoning me?"

"Why are you punishing me so?"

"I hate you!!!"

"Its your fault for allowing me to leave your side and enter into such a place of loneliness and pain."

As Source, I could not leave you, yet as All That Is, I could not join a dream of separation. So I left a little bit of sanity within your insane dream to guide you out of it when that is what you would desire.

So lovingly I let you dream insanely until a time when you would ask of me to help you waken from this dream of isolation, abandonment, pain and suffering. You are asking NOW, and I am bringing all the insanity within this dream for you to see and for you to allow to fade into the nothingness from which it came so you can gently follow all your guides back home to the place within my Sacred Heart you never really left.

I love you soooo and you have never offended me no matter what appearances may seem to be,

The Voice for Love"

Observing this Phenomenon

Allowing other's desires to manifest does not mean I must share these desires with them. Other's reactions to me as if this lack of joining is somehow an attack upon them is just the reflection of my own essential desire to experience separation from God and then existentially turned away from Him accusing Him of abandoning me.

michael

THE MYSTERY OF GOD'S PRESENCE

god is…

therefore, god is a mystery, an ever unfolding mystery

where we live eternally experiencing the depths

of the love god is… deeper and deeper forever…

to experience mystery one must surrender…

surrender allows the mystery to show itself to us

it allows god to "be seen" even whilst you abide yet
in time…

mystery and symbol go hand in hand whilst you
abide in time

surrender to the ever flowing love of the mystery of what
is…… god, abba!

the key to knowing god is to love unconditionally…

see only innocence in all things and always desire that
which is of the highest good of all

why are these so important?

EVERYTHING you see is YOU, the depths of love and
innocence you can see and feel in another's soul

you experience as yourself…

the deeper you love yourself unconditionally, the more and
more you see your innocence, you will recognize it
in another…

125

surrender to the innocence and the mystery of creation
and then you will receive miracles…

not always of this world but within the symbols that the
gift of grace descends upon you that point to
home eternally

denisa/jeshua

mystery of Self

i am the very mystery i explore.

i experience the very heart of my Self

in all that is before me.

in reaching out to another i touch my Self.

in taking in the beauty that surrounds me

i embrace my Self.

the unfoldment of life

is the very unfoldment of my Self...

in experience with Self.

grace is the path i walk

as i bless the Self i meet

in everyone and everything.

the small self surrenders unconditionally

to Grace.....to Love.....to the Father.....

to All That Is.

anne

what joy!

my allowing all in a space of love for all
and then surrendering any control over
what is revealed in the space before me
is thrilling
is joyous
is delightful
the mystery of it all is only seen
by my allowing it to be what it truly is

michael

HEAVEN IS A THOUGHT AWAY

heaven, my sweet one is not a place....

it izzzzzzzzz a state of being...

when you hear the wind chimes playing their melody of
song...

a feeling of heaven...

when you look at the smiling faces within the most
beautiful sun flower...

a feeling of heaven...

music that lifts your soul...

a feeling of heaven...

my beautiful one heaven is a feeling chosen by *you* NOW...

in these days there will be much you can put your
attention on that will not bring a feeling of heaven...

you will choose...

you are the creator in every now moment

you will choose

is this not like choosing heaven or hell?

love or trust?

you are the chooser, my dear one...

all that appears to be "hell" is heaven on it's way...

you allow what is not of love in your world to die, so that I can replace it all

with sun flowers

so, bless what is "falling" and go play….

yes, please just go and play, laugh, dance, sing hug, frolic and bless it all…

THE VOICE FOR LOVE thru denisa

i live in my story…..

remaining true to the plot line of separation that i choose

until i awaken to the possibility of another story.

this other story brings me hope,

yet i need courage and conviction to move out of the old and into the new remembered story.

separation is what i have immersed myself in for so long.

in comparison, the 'new' story seems so far-fetched, and yet it feels soooooo good when it comes as a thought to my mind.

i love the story of heaven and who i am.

i love seeing all as love coming to me.

and i love remembering i am here to love

all that is unlike love....

i love to remember that this is my creation,

and that i call myself home by remembering to love all.

anne

THE EYE OF THE STORM

be as the eye of the storm…

in the middle of the surrounding chaotic energies is the calm center contained within the eye…

you are the "eye."

stay in this place of peace and "allow" all around you to be as it is knowing it is perfection…

all events are neutral…

you can perceive them in any way you so desire, this is your free will

however, once true peace is "known, truly known" it becomes you,

you have walked the bridge of allowance, whose destination is the gift of knowing that every moment is wrapped in the petals of the rose of god…

yes, you KNOW that all is love, you have witnessed it…

therefore, the gift is yours, it is the gift of grace…

knowledge is remembered as you have created a space for love to enter by the very choice for allowance… once this peace is known you are home…

then you abide as the eye and radiate the peace contained within this center to all of creation…

the gift of allowance has bestowed upon you this knowledge,

it is the gift of grace…

now, be the peace… walk it, talk it, drink it, sleep it,

BE IT

I love you so,

jeshua/denisa

PLANT A "SON" FLOWER

Denisa and Michael here dialogue with Jeshua who speaks
of patiently planting the seeds of love and allowing them to
grow in their own time as we nurture and protect these
seeds through our thoughts of sharing and giving.

good morning, sweet one, I see within each of your hearts

and I witness mine....

within our shared heart there lives a most beautiful garden

and its soil is deep, rich and bountiful...

it is waiting this day for you to go within and plant a seed
that has been waiting for your attention for eons of time...

it is liken to a "son" flower, it is yours and yours alone,

your own unique, perfect seed of Christ...

close your eyes, take your awareness within your
heart center...

you will find it there

now I ask of you to water it with your loving thoughts
once each day...

the flowers from this seed are magical...

they are of colors unseen on earth...

they carry a vibration that extends a golden light wherever
they appear

with oh, so much love,

Jeshua,

The Voice for Love thru denisa

our garden of delight

thank you, dear jeshua, for reminding us that
each of us carries the seed of the son of God

which we can allow to be planted…
we need but take this thought into our heart
where it is placed as a willingness
to love and to know the love we are,
to see and to be love in our perceived world,
where this seed will grow and bloom
into flowers of many colors and hues
for all to enjoy and delight in their beauty

michael

patiently sitting in bliss

surrendering to love
allows the desire of your heart for peace
to manifest in its own time
no need to teach
no need to preach
no need to try to convince
just sitting in bliss as love and willing to see only love
with the surety that the awesomely formidable power
source we call love
is ever present
and will provide at the right time and in the right place
for all to receive what they need

jeshua/michael

as ONE

thank you michael

and one we are...
denisa

grace's voiceless whisperings

life becomes so full when all you see is love
even what at first glance appears not so like love
when offered to the voice for love within
is transmuted to a loving feeling
connected to a loving thought

137

spirit sent with grace's voiceless whisperings

michael

denesa asks:

"why is it so important to think only loving thoughts?"

jeshua responds:

"my dear one, you are all one connected within a heart yet
unseen but *felt*
that is forever more in this your earth plane…

you may not see this or be aware that this is so, but trust
me it izzzzzzzzz so…

as you go within and send out loving thoughts, or thoughts
of peace or simply a s-m-i-l-e, that feeling is immediately
felt by all…

and you will begin to notice that all aspects of yourself will
start showing up differently…

maybe a little softer around the edges, maybe more
peaceful, maybe more open to dialogue about
love's presence…

so you see, this is how we lift the whole, with our
loving thoughts…

they emit an energy that sings to all the song of home,

an energy that is the very life force you breathe…

it expands and expansion is creation…

it is the truth of your beingness…

think often of the love I carry for you, you are loved
beyond worldly thinking…

this very thought, this knowingness expands into the all of
creation…

with that,

I bid you adieu,

jeshua/denisa

THE GARDEN

Here, Denisa speaks of the garden of awareness within our 3D world. Through a willingness to root up all that is unlike love and see it for what it is... the illusion stemming from our false belief in separation, we ascend into our true presence as the creator of our world: a world where we experience "a field or ocean of awareness" while we witness the presence of love as seamless and eternal.

Within the garden, as you are willing to examine the roots of false beliefs that bring forth experience unlike love, you come to the truth of your being... your I AM PRESENCE...

Yes, even the energies of Jeshua fall away as they too ascend into the I AM.

This is the journey within the kingdom... the realization that I AM my own universe... that all within it is either reflecting my belief that only love is real or allowing me to witness a belief still carried deep within the soil of my garden that is not the truth of that which I Am...

That being said, my beloved, it is time to take responsibility for your own universe... YOU ARE the ocean of love...there is nothing else! Yet the veil, the illusion, will show itself in many ways... as you move into your I AM PRESENCE the power you extend into

the illusion is the very power of love... there is no other power!

When you use the power of love to BLESS ALL UNLIKE
LOVE ITSELF appearing in your universe you transform
it… thus, you ascend more and more into your
I AM presence…

this process is eternal whether in body or not, you are
eternally experiencing the love that this I AM PRESENCE
embodies…. forever and ever this is your sojourn… all you
need do

is proclaim that which YOU ARE… and you are

ABBA

you are GOD

ONE WITH ALL THAT IS… forever EXPERIENCING

be-coming

the grandness

of that which you are eternally… a field of awareness
witnessing the mystery

of love's eternal presence

denisa

surrender

i close my eyes

and surrender my entire being

to the Voice for Love.

i see all that is unlike love

coming out from within me

and placing it on a silver tray.

i hand it to my beloved Self

who takes what i have created

in separation and innocence

and transforms it all into

pure love....its original state.

i feel clear and released

from the bondage of disowned creations,

and i now know the Truth of all i see.

anne

VOICES BLOOMING WITHIN
THE STAIRCASE

Bless all that you see and hear and know that you are but blessing yourself. You need no outside savior to return you to your true Home. The Bridge to Home is laid out before you as you willingly allow and bless all.

I spoke with you of the staircase of ascension… you meet all of your-selves with each step you take each has its voice!

Thus, as you blossom into the next step, each voice will be left behind… until you reach your I AM VOICE and that voice is eternally extending its mystery into your beingness

Bless each of these voices for I say unto you they are you… a belief still held within the mind appearing in form… some of these voices speak to you of "others" who would come to "save" you… only you can remember YOU. There will be no other!

Belief births form…. choosing that which you believe to be true is your destiny… choose only love to be true…

denisa

The Eternal Blossom

you are forever

the eternal blossom

born of the seed

of that which you are

GOD…

denisa

the passing of one blossom
lays the seeds for future blooming
as all is unfolding for the benefit of all

michael

My Now of The Past

i allow the past to become my Now…

to bless what comes and give it to Love.

in this conscious moment,

painful memories transform before me,

as Love shows me the Truth.

and now.....the past.....

made new in the light of Love....

dwells in the peace of my Holy Mind.

Anne

THE SEA OF NOT KNOWING

The sea of not knowing...

where I do not know what anything is or is for

emerges for me as a new way of being...

where flow replaces agenda

where time is not even a thought.

The living of life is transformed within me,

and can only be described as living/being

in the absolute NOW.

The sea of not knowing...bewildering at first...

as I seek to be oriented in the grayness of my mind...

The usual markers (beliefs) are gone,

as the thought comes that I know not what anything is or
is for.

"How shall I proceed," I ask my Self.

"Wait. Be still. Breathe into the moment,

and you will know, beloved, without doubt.

You will feel it in your heart center,

and the knowing of action or non-action

147

will be self-evident…without question."

The sea of not knowing ushers me into a new reality

where only Love exists.

And as I hold this single thought:

only Love exists,

acceptance and allowance naturally extend from me

in each moment…the eternal NOW…the only moment,

and blessing all becomes my only purpose.

anne

THE MESSAGE OF THE BIRD'S SONG

Jeshua tells us that, incredible as it may seem, we are the creator of our world, all of it. He asks that we allow the old world of strife and struggle to fall away and to enjoy the songs of the birds. We have created these birds to sing to and for us of the joy of being. Nothing else is necessary for our happiness but to listen with thanks and appreciation for our creative power granted in grace by the Creator of it all

this day see with a new eye, hear with a new ear…

the birds are singing a song just for you, yes, just for you…

it is called "hear my song."

the words to this song are simple…

we are singing your praises, we are singing of the love we have for you,

for all of creation has come as a thought from within you

the sun comes from within you as does our song, as does the sky, the stars and all that you see.

we are all here for you… this is the song we sing every morn

we sing it… will you hear it?

all that has been birthed that is unlike this song is falling away now!

so, sing it with us today….

love yourself, remember yourself as we know you to be
you are "All that is"…

come and sing with us for a new morn is upon you!

THE VOICE FOR LOVE,

Jeshua thru denisa

Universes Are Born Of My Desire

universes are born of my desire.

it is the sweet Self of my being

the very power of the Creative Source flowing thru me

that allows the birthing of all I desire to create.

the awakened heart hears the song of Love

and joins with joy-filled voice

to remember and reawaken the Christ.

anne/Love

ALLOW THE STORM

Jeshua here uses the ocean to make an analogy of our changing moods and circumstances. He notes how all of it is perfect when seen through the eyes of love. None of it is to be feared. None of it is to be unwanted. All of it is necessary to bring us home to the beauty and joy of our One Self, the I Am Presence of Love.

you know those days when you witness an ocean so calm that seagulls appear as if they are enjoying a relaxing bath …

you also know those days when the storm approaches and the winds are howling and waves are churning and crashing upon the shore of life

yet, the ocean is always the ocean… whether calm or stormy it is still "the ocean"

whatever is happening around it does not change it's ocean ness…

the ocean allows the calm…it also allows the storms to blow through for it knows that the storm will bring waters to the shores that birth abundant life…

the crashing waves take back grains of sand that long to spend some time in the ocean once again only to appear on the shores another day…

they are ready to come home…

all of it is perfection...

I would ask of you now to be as the ocean... allow the calm moments to bring you rest and rejuvenation allow the storms to blow through you...

bless them as they pass for they bring much, much good to the shores they land upon... bless what is leaving and bless what is coming...

I AM THE VOICE FOR LOVE

Jeshua thru denisa

BLESS ALL

bless what is leaving......

bless what is coming.......

know only Oneness in all of it

for, in Truth,

that is all there is.

love,

anne

THE SIMPLE PLAN

See but love.

Be but Love.

Give to all.

To have all.

michael

ALIGNING WITH LOVE

your world as you know it has changed…

allow me to say that it is moving into a very new dimension…

abundance within your life will be given unto you as you extend love…

where you give love you will receive your daily bread…

you need do nothing but extend love…

all, ALL that is out of alignment with love will fall away… it must leave…

the energies unlike love no longer can exist for there is no-thing for them to hold onto…

yes, your world has changed count it all as good…

I AM THE VOICE FOR LOVE

thru denisa

Extend Love

changes abound,

and Love stands firm

knowing this is the time

for all unlike Love

to be transmuted.

extend yourself to all others.

extend that which you are without fear.

for it is in Love

that we know the secret to Life.

it is in Love

that abundance becomes our reality.

Love

anne

ALL IS

In ACIM Jesus says, there is only one problem, "the thought of separation" and only one solution, "the thought of unity." Yet, we insist on discussing it, elaborating about it and explaining it, when all we need do is to try it. Here we are asked to allow all else to be exactly as it is without criticism, correction or complaint. In so doing, we unite all things.

all is al-ways perfect… what keeps one from this
realization is the ego……… (the thought of separation
made manifest)

The Voice for Love, thru denisa

All is al-ways perfect. how simple… how easy this
statement feels, yet it is in the living of it that it's profound
basis is recognized. All is perfect. There is nothing to do….
nothing to fix…. All is al-ways perfect…this is my Truth
by choice.

anne

Within the knowingness that comes with patience there
is no outcome since all is known as instantaneous.
Outcomes depend upon a thought of separation and
knowingness just IS.

michael

Attachment to Outcome

when one moves into their I AM PRESENCE you abide in a
dimension where

ALL IS…

a field of awareness that observes and blesses creation all
is perfection…

thus, while you still abide on the earth plane you now see
all things

within your I AM knowing-ness…

you abide with no attachment to any outcome for you
know that all is al-ways perfect

now you live in freedom…

observing and dancing as creation continues to
birth itself…

always birthing the perfection of itself

denisa

JUST FOR TODAY

Not just endless sky do I see but the simple solution to all perceived problems. I see the unity of love within all.

just for today would you see yourself as the blue of the endless sky?

our union eternal....

watch with me as some clouds pass by, simply observe them, even bless them if you would like...

now, go and play, go and en-joy your day for your "real work" is done...

The Voice for Love, thru denisa

oh, i just love this so much....

watching the sky....

observing the clouds....

seeing oneness...

feeling oneness...

blessing the beauty of it all

what wonderful work for today!

and now... i can play!!

anne

Love's Presence

look out to the horizon's edge......

the endless sky speaks:

enter here this blissful space

as clouds blithely glide past

simple, quiet, glorious.

sky......clouds.....endless perfection.......

they all exist in a consciousness

that knows only peace.

here, in this picture of serenity

Love breathes in and out

the power of presence in the Now.

Love/anne

grace's voiceless whisperings

life becomes so full when all you see is love
even what at first glance appears not so like love
when offered to the voice for love within
is transmuted to a loving feeling
connected to a loving thought
spirit sent with grace's voiceless whisperings

michael

And once again we ask:

"why is it so important to think only loving thoughts?"

The answer is the same my dear one, you are all one
connected within a heart yet unseen but *felt*

that is forever more in this your earth plane

you may not see this or be aware that this is so

trust me.........it izzzzzzzzz so

as you go within and send out loving thoughts, or thoughts
of peace or simply a s-m-i-l-e...

that feeling is immediately felt by all...

and you will begin to notice that all aspects of yourself will
start showing up differently

maybe a little softer around the edges, maybe more
peaceful, maybe more open to dialogue

159

about love's presence…

so you see, this is how we lift the whole, with our loving thoughts…

they emit an energy that sings to all the song of home

an energy that is the very life force you breathe…

it expands and expansion is creation…

it is the truth of your beingness

think often of the love I carry for you

you are loved beyond wordly thinking…

this very thought, this knowingness expands into the all of creation

with that

I bid you adieu,

jeshua/denisa

BE AT PEACE, DEAR ONE
OF MY HEART

Just as the Beatles sang, "In times of trouble, Mother Mary comes to me, singing words of wisdom "Let it Be, Let it Be," Mother Mary here likens us to the whole earth birthing the new world of unity and love for all. The apparent pain will turn to joy.

Just as we allow the birth of a child to come in its own time in the world of duality, the birth of this new earth will start in pain and end in the joy of love and unity of spirit.

I bring with me radiant colors of purple, gold
and turquoise.

I come to fill your auric field with colors of such magnitude
that you radiate their essence where ever you may find
yourself in any moment…

I bring with me the everlasting love of the Holy Mother…

I bring with me peace, joy and good news…

I would like to go back in time, just for a moment…

My "son" was birthed to the world as a most radiant being
of light who came with a mission to "die" to the
unreal world…

allowing all to witness eternal life…

Yet, I, as a mother, endured much grief to bring this miracle to the world…

My grief was temporal, the miracle unending…

I carry within me the knowingness of the unconditional love of the Holy Mother, the compassion, the deep, deep trust that love is ever present, and that I am that love as are you, my beloved "son" of holy mother earth…

I come to you this day to speak with you of a mission…

This mission is lifting the beloved mother earth into a new dimension, a new earth…

This new baby is coming, it is here, yet not birthed into your view from earthly

eyes as of yet…

You are all the womb of this birth…

Before every birth of the precious child the mother experiences labor pains, does she not….?

Yet, right before the birth of the precious one, the pains get a little quicker, a little more painful….

Yet, once the baby is born, the mother cries with joy…

Remember these words of comfort in your next of days for I love you so……..

You are doing a most marvelous job of birthing your new world,

one that brings with it all of the radiance of your
true home…

Unending waters of clear crystal beauty, friends and family
frolicking in the abundance of light and love struggle will be
a thing of the past

joy will be your ever lasting experience…

I am but a thought away come to me when you desire, and
I will bless you

comfort you and hold you in my arms as my

new born "babe."

Think of me often and know that all is well and that you
are soooooooo loved and watched over…

carry peace within your heart

with love

Mother Mary thru denisa

THE SHIFT OF THE AGES

The second coming of the Christ was promised in what seems, in our dualistic perception, to be many ages ago. In reality, it occurred simultaneously with the promise made. In time, it appears as if NOW all are awakening to this Christhood, even those who seem to be apart from love's presence. It is for those who are open to this Presence of Love in all things to receive it and acknowledge it to and for all the world. This is the I Am Presence we speak of here in as many different ways as are necessary so that all will hear this message of universal Love.

Embarking on your shores is the GOLDEN ERA.

I speak to this "one" often, for she surrenders herself to me with every living breath...

I have prepared her and many others who were willing to hear me for what is now on the shores of this your beloved earth...

Thus, I come again, a promise kept.

You will not see me in the physical as a man but you will recognize me in many others in the coming of days...

I spoke many times of this your moment on earth where only love would be seen, witnessed and shared...

Many on your earth plane now are carrying within their physical bodies such a high particulate of light that your earth has been heating, thus, your global warming...

This light is bringing up for all to see that which is unlike it, only for one purpose....to be healed, transmuted and then forgotten like a dream that never existed.

See all these changes as good: the ice caps melting, the chaos in your government and your economy, for all that is unlike love will be replaced with all that is of love...

You will witness many miracles, you will "feel" from the depths of your being that all is well, though your earthly eyes may not see this holy vision...

Place this vision within your heart, and see that all of it is love... all is energy, and the energy of love has come to bring all unlike it back into the heart.

Each one on your beloved planet and those unseen are here to ring in this golden era.... bless the one's who have held energies that will need to be released as you bless the one's who carry the living light...........

I leave you now with peace and I shower you with many heartfelt hugs from home...

~namaste~

JESHUA, THE HEART OF Love

thru denisa

WHY PATIENCE?

as you bless all that you see
it is necessary to have patience…
patience builds power…
real power
the only power…
the power of love!!!!!
as you continue to bless
even that which appears
as the fog hiding the beauty
of the crystal blue-green ocean
your power grows…
your responsibility to bless grows…
and the very power of love
will bring miracles…
and patience
will allow love
to show itself to you…
it will bring you many
ahhhhhhhh moments…
the very power of the blessing
brings all things home
to the truth of that which
it truly issssss……
LOVE
~DENISA~

Why patience you ask?

Patience flows from trust,
trust in the power of life to extend itself for the benefit of
all.
Trust becomes your way of being when you know yourself
as united to all as the One creation of the One Creator
God, Abba.
Trust becomes your way of being when you know yourself
as an extension of a loving thought from this Creator.
Trust becomes your way of being as you release all
attachment to outcomes, knowing so clearly that you, from
your limited perspective, can never know what anything
truly is or is for.
So, patiently allow all to unfold in the joy of knowing that
you are abundantly provided for by a loving Creator. It
always was so and always will be so.

michael

i look within myself to find patience
as a way of being in each moment of my life.
it is patience i call upon when life unfolds
and challenge presents itself to me.

patience lies in trust, i see,
for it is in trusting the perfection of all life
that allows me to be patient in time
accepting that what comes is exactly what's needed.

steadfast in patience and trust....
i bless every moment without question,
and in time i experience the gift of joy and wonder
in how all events ultimately... lovingly serve all.
anne

THESE WORDS ARE BUT TEACHING TOOLS

the goal of any teaching tool is to ever so slowly undo the
earth mind...
all teaching tools are temporal as even these words you
have
placed your beautiful eyes upon are merely a symbol of a
thought materializing in time and space...
that thought taken by me is to extend only the
atonement....
wo-laaaaa ( ) this appears...
mystery.......
my desire to extend the atonement sent out a vibrational
field that this one known as denisa
matched in her desire to awaken...
thus, she now extends that very same desire, together
with jeshua...
and many are being "drawn" to witness these words for
they re-cog-nize them...
they spark a remembrance somewhere deep within that
will burst open a seed that has been dormant
waiting to be remembered again...
today, I would like to speak to you about the energy that is
behind these particular words
that form in time and space from an energy named jeshua
we come forth from the dimension of 33
we are one divine light expressing ourselves, our energies
joined from a "field" that
can be felt but not yet quite "seen" by you
I, as jesus, am one with other energies of this dimension
we are one with Christ,

Christ consciousness,
abba, all that is...
the vibration that exists behind these words and within
them is an energy of awakening...
there is much, much going on behind these words that you
cannot yet quite grasp....
we are all a part of you whom you have called to yourself
out of your de-sire to awaken...
yes, my beloved, your de-sire brought this expression of
love to you...
ponder that deeply, it is your desire that brought
this to you
nothing, no-thing can show up in time and space that you
have not called to yourself...
maybe not in a conscious state, but within you you have
asked for it....
in truth, it is you coming to you, this is how powerful
you are...
this is why I say desire only the at-one-ment
oh, I hear those other desires that live in your heart...
yet all those will be birthed as you desire only the
atonement for what is lying underneath all
earthly desires is in truth this union...
you are looking for it outside of yourself....
finding it within is the goal
you *are* the goal.... sweet one
as you we come to you to sprinkle you with loving
energies of home and we are with you now
therefore, home is but a thought away
and you are that "very" thought........
peace be with you,
jeshua/denisa

i share this goal

and have long held it consciously
as my one purpose for this life in our world of duality
i feel the truth conveyed in your words
without questioning their authenticity and authority
i thank you for the willingness to patiently await
my passing through the ring of fear
to openly express and cultivate the love
i know myself to be
in union with your energies
dear jeshua,
i love you soooo,

michael

jeshua responds:

your beauty is beyond words that could be expressed...
thank you, for your willingness..
and now a final message unto you...

the eye of the needle is passed through when you bring
within you even the energies of jeshua,
for they have been you bringing you home
bring us home with you now
with that we bid you adieu,
the heart of love

anne contributes to the conversation:

it is my desire for love that brings love to me.

the words.....the people....the places.....the very energy of
love
calls me out of my self that i may see my Self.
i am cause and effect.
i am the thought, the thinker, and the result.
i am the writer, producer, director and actor.
to know this at the core of my being is to come home.
there is only the One.
All is One.

and now....we come home
to the Light that we are.
to pass thru the eye of the needle
is to know only Oneness
no names.....no identities.....
only Oneness.
jeshua/anne

AS ONE

utter trust in our endeavors is present for me
as we walk as one through the eye of the needle
no fear expressed in needing to identify
what is me, what is you, what you say, what i say, who you
are, what i am, what you have, what i have, what you have
done, what i have done
within the eye there is no you, there is no me
when i say jeshua a feeling of truth and power engulfs me
i unabashedly proclaim i am at cause of all and all is good
and all is love
my joy overflows upon all i see, all i hear, all i experience
dancing and singing in the streets is proclaimed as my way
of being
all else that is not joy and love and fun dissolves in the light
of my love

jeshua/michael/denisa/anne as one

in response to what denisa has written:

the eye of the needle...

the small eye meets the ONE

I have spoken before of the journey to the kingdom

I am now speaking to you about the journey within it of
the needle to enjoy the fruits of this union

the journey within is one of steadfastness...

175

responsibility for every thought

you see, my dear one all is within you

there is nothing outside of you

you now are creating your outer world with your thoughts

and there is only love…

all that you see now is the light…

if it appears otherwise it is a "veil" that is coming from a thought contained within you

and it is the small you….

thoughts carried deep within, such as unworthiness, being unlovable, needing to be seen, needing to be recognized

(the small self always wants to

be seen, noticed, recognized

and puffed up")

your old self can no longer be seen now

it no longer exists

you are walking light, one with me….

as you witness these projections, I would ask of you to come within ask of me

what is this for?

how did I create this experience?

I say unto you the one in front of you is Jeshua, all is jeshua

appearing to you exactly as you believe yourself to be...

I would ask of you who do YOU choose to be? the little
self or the I AM...

there is only light, yet the duality is contained within you
and the shadow

small self is also within you...

you are here to transform this shadow self

if you have a moment, a moment of reaction to anything
you see, it is the little you not seeing all as perfect...

so come to me

create a space for me to come and show you how you are
creating that which brings you unhappiness, fear and all
the rest

embrace the moment, for not to embrace is to resist

and resistance brings more of the same

so, embrace when you witness the seed within that has
brought forth your creation

embrace it with love bring it into your heart center and let
it flow through your front heart and out through the back
of your heart chakra...

now, you have loved it and transmuted it

only love heals, dear one...

you are dissolving the small self into the grand self as you embrace the shadow

with love…

there is no longer time for you to believe that what you see outside of you is not coming from within you

take responsibility for all thoughts…

judgment will bring you

an experience of the same…

not seeing all things as perfect

will bring more experiences

unlike love… fear and lack and the belief in them are coming from inside you… let them go, transmute them, trust in love, live within the eye and allow all around you to be "exactly" as it is

think your loving thoughts, water your garden with thoughts of joy, laughter, song and dance

see through the veil, my love, for behind every moment

I am there…

see only me within all now's!

I love you sooooo,

Jeshua

the voice for love

CHOICE

Free Will does not mean that we get to choose the curriculum we must learn. We are only free to choose the time when we will awaken. When we do choose to awaken, time is no more, duality and all separation disappear. We willingly allow all. We willingly bless all.

Simplicity 101

One problem

"The thought of separation"

Conflict

Disease

Death

One solution

"The Thought of unity"

Peace

Well-being

Eternal life

Your only choice

CHOICE

your eternal freedom…

when an aspect of you

"leaves'

as you have chosen

for love…

bless it…

for the choice

is an aspect of you

yet still

choosing

to play in duality…

free will

my beloved…

honor all those

who choose differently from you…

for they are a part of you

eternal and radiant

yet choosing

to play in the game

of time…

duality

and they too

will come home

to their truth…

ME…

in their perfect moment…

all I ask of you

is to bless them

from your I AM PRESENCE

THEN

allow them to play

in a dimension of creation

until they too

choose only love

THAT WHICH I AM…..

~denisa~

THE SECOND COMING
TRUTH

The truth is true

We are one

The truth is true

We are invulnerable

The truth is true

We are

Nothing else is true

simplicity is so appealing

in a world i make of complications and distress

i will to let all go

surrendering from where it came

a place of fear

a place of shame

a place of regret and guilt

a place alone

a place of sadness and pain

to be replaced by love
as the light of your simple message shines through the
darkened lens

projecting SIMPLICITY upon my mistaken world

michael

THE WINDOWS OF YOUR SOUL

within each of you is a diamond crystal …

a perfect aspect of the ONE

thru the windows of this crystal you witness your reality

eternally…

the process of coming home is the very process of
wiping free

any last traces of shadow that have blurred the clearness

of your view as you gaze upon your universe…

your personal universe…

when you live in surrender you step back from this
magic crystal

that brings forth your every moment…

you no longer "take" thoughts that create worlds
upon worlds

of distortion…

NOW…

you are the observer of the "gifts" that appear as you gaze
through it

each now moment…

as the observer you have stated to ME that you have
returned to your

original state...
knowing that I the I AM of you
I bring to you every breath you take
every site you see
every experience you witness...

Now, you journey "within the kingdom"
there is nowhere to seek for you have found...
no questions to ask for now you KNOW
that all is ME...

NOW you allow ME to bring you the "gifts from home"...
you know that your every desire is heard and felt by me
and that all is brought to you in its perfect time
in its perfect moment
just for you!!!

yes, it is all ME/YOU coming and going...

you allow all to be as it is...
whatever appears is there only for you from ME...

whatever "seemingly" is not there
is perfect and to be blessed and surrendered...

for would not I bring you only perfection????

no longer do you create with the thoughts of the little self...

your loving thoughts
your blessings
now create your universe...

you rest in my arms
windows clear and clean
and allow life
to come to you

you bless it all and know that your purpose is not to be
the doer and the maker but to allow ME
to bring you perfect reflections
of that which "you" believe to be true
in any moment...

now you witness the fruits of your thoughts in form in
your life
with the wonder of the
little child...

As you now "observe" all things you have melded into our
oneness...

you have stepped back from what you thought was life

and allowed me to bring you "real life"...

keep your windows pristine and clear in this way only...

bless all that you see…
be grateful for love's presence…
extend your palms each morning
and value re-ceiving
the gifts of grace that will descend
into your holy mind…
allow all unloving thoughts
to ascend back into ME
thus
continually receiving more and more
of ME…

I AM the highest part of you
that loves you beyond all worlds
of form…

I AM bringing the mystery of my love deeper and deeper
into your very earth existence…

this is the second coming…
walking on earth
as ME
with ME
for ME
extending ME/YOU
wherever you find our Self to be…

with that
I bid you adieu

denisa/jeshua

THE GOAL

the goal of all teaching tools is to bring you to
a space whilst in time where you "know"
you are god...
where you come to know that as god,
you are constantly creating your reality
and to take responsibility for your creations...

not to judge them
yet to wonder about them
as the little child looks in awe
at all that he sees...

to rest in humility
not knowing what a thing is
or what it is for
and to ask in that space of humility
to be shown how it came to be...

the power of thought
is faster than the speed of light...
it creates worlds upon worlds

as you, my beloveds
come to own your creations
and lift your thoughts to one with the mind of Christ
there will be no more distortions

there will be only heaven

so, start at the end…

knowing you are one with the

mind and heart of Christ…

you are god in body

and you are the creator

of worlds unending.…

what would you wish to create???

become unlimited in thinking,

breathing in and seeing

only the presence of love…

Jeshua/denisa